MW01027038

Also by Blanche Knott:

The Worst of Truly Tasteless Jokes
Truly Tasteless Doctor Jokes
Truly Tasteless Lawyer Jokes
Truly Tasteless Cube Calendar 1991
Truly Tasteless Joke-A-Date Calendar 1991
Truly Tasteless Anatomy Jokes, Vols. I and II
Truly Tasteless Jokes, Vols. I–X

The Very Worst of Truly Tasteless Jokes

The Very Worst of Truly Tasteless Jokes

Blanche Knott

St. Martin's Press
New York

 For information, address St. Martin's Press, 175 Fifth Avenue, New York, N.Y. 10010.

Library of Congress Cataloging-in-Publication Data
Knott, Blanche.
The very worst of truly tasteless jokes / by Blanche Knott.
p. cm.
"A Thomas Dunne book."
ISBN 0-312-05185-9
1. American wit and humor. I. Title.
PN6162.K618 1990
818'.5402—dc20 90-37315
CIP

First Edition: November 1990

10 9 8 7 6 5 4 3 2 1

For Luke,
who had to find out too

Contents

Ethnic Variegated

How many Ethiopians can you fit in a bathtub?

I don't know—they keep slipping down the drain.

□ □ □

A nice Italian boy was raised by his very strict mama, who forced him to promise not to marry an American girl. "You cannot trust them," she lectured her son time after time. "They cannot cook, they are no good in bed, and they will call you names, names to insult you like dago, wop, guinea. You hear me, Tony?"

"Yes, Mama," said Tony obediently, but over the years he learned to tune out her litany. Indeed, when he turned twenty-one he realized his mother's worst fears by marrying an American girl.

"Tony, Tony," she wailed, "you'll never be able to trust her—"

"No, Mama, you've got the Americans all wrong," interrupted her son. "Tania is a good cook, she's great in bed, and she only calls me a dago when I call her a nigger."

□ □ □

What's so great about getting a blow job from an Ethiopian woman?

You know she'll drink every drop.

□ □ □

What do Mexicans call Bartles & Jaymes wine cooler?
Dos Okies.

□ □ □

Sergeant Mack had a fine time during his stay in Hong Kong, but paid for it when he came down with a strange Oriental venereal disease. So he made the rounds of every American doctor in the community. To his horror he discovered that not only were they unable to cure him, they all informed him that the only course of treatment was to have his penis amputated.

Desperate, Sergeant Mack made an appointment with a leading Chinese doctor, figuring that he might know more about an Eastern malady. "Do you, Doctor Cheung, think I need to have my dick amputated?" he asked anxiously.

"No, no, no," replied the Chinese doctor testily.

A huge smile broke out over the serviceman's face. "Boy, that's *great*, Doc. Every one of those American medics said they'd have to cut it off."

"Those Western doctors—all they ever want to do is cut, cut, cut," explained Dr. Cheung exasperatedly. "You just wait two weeks. Penis fall off all by itself."

□ □ □

Fred was the manager for a construction project in downtown Rochester and he requested bids from local construction companies. The first interview was with a representative from Kowalski Brothers.

"You've seen the plans," said Fred. "How much'll you charge to get the work done?"

"Two hundred thousand dollars," said the Pole.

"Reasonable," commented Fred. "What's the breakdown?"

"One hundred thousand for materials, one hundred thousand for labor."

"Okay," said Fred, jotting down the bid and showing him to the door, "I'll get back to you."

The next interview was with Gennaro Rossellini of Fratelli Rossellini, who came up with a four-hundred-thousand-dollar bid. "Half for labor, half for materials," he explained.

"That's a little high," Fred told him, "but I'll get back to you."

The third bid came in from Ben Cohen of Cohen Construction. Calculating quickly, he offered, "Six hundred thousand dollars."

"Jesus, that's high," exclaimed Fred. "Could you break that down for me?"

"You bet. Two hundred grand for me, two hundred grand for you, and two hundred grand for the Pole."

□ □ □

An Englishman, a Frenchman, and an American were captured by Indians and taken back to their camp, where it soon became apparent that they were to be dealt with mercilessly. The Indian chief did, however, offer them the weapon of their choice with which to kill themselves.

"A pistol," requested the Englishman. "God Save the Queen," he pronounced, then blew his brains out. His companions watched in horror as the Indians flayed him and proceeded to make his skin into a canoe.

"Next?" inquired the chief.

The Frenchman asked for a sabre. "*Vive la France*," he gasped as he disembowled himself and sank to the ground. The remaining captive again watched as the corpse was skinned and made into a canoe.

"And you, Yankee?" asked the chief.

"A fork," demanded the American. Grasping it with both hands, he proceeded to stab himself wildly, shrieking, "So much for your fucking canoe!"

□ □ □

How many Italians does it take to screw in a light bulb?

Two. One to screw it in and one to shoot the witnesses.

□ □ □

Two Italians are walking down the street when one turns to the other and says, "Nunzio, you know, there's-a one time I really like to have-a sex."

"When is-a that, Mario?" asked his friend.

"Jus' before I have-a cigaretta."

□ □ □

Hear about the guy who was half Jewish and half Japanese?

He was circumcised at Benny Hannah's.

□ □ □

Why did God create armadillos?

So Mexicans would have something to eat on the half-shell.

□ □ □

"I tell you, sir, this is a great country and I praise God that I came over," the Irishman was expounding to a new acquaintance. "Where else, I ask you, could it happen that you could do a hard day's work, then find yourself outside the gates, standing in the rain, waiting for the bus—"

"You call that great?" queried the man next to him at the bar.

"Ah, but wait now. A big black limousine pulls up,

and the boss opens the back door and says, 'It's a hell of a night to be out in the rain. Why don't you come in here and warm up?' And when you're inside, he says, 'That coat's awfully wet—let me buy you a new one, all right?' And after that he asks where you live and says, 'That's a long drive on a night like this, why not come to my house?' So he takes you to his big mansion and gives you a big meal and a few drinks and a warm bed for the night and a hot breakfast and a ride back to work. I tell you, this is a great country. It would never happen to me in Ireland."

"And this really happened to you here?" asked his acquaintance skeptically.

"No. But happened to my sister."

□ □ □

What do you have when ten boat people go over a cliff in a Lincoln Continental?

A damn shame—you can fit ten of them in a Hyundai.

□ □ □

What does an Ethiopian woman never say to her husband?

"Eat me, darling."

□ □ □

It so happened that Myron and Vinnie came of age at the same time. From his father, Vinnie received a brand-new handgun, while at his Bar Mitzvah on the other side of town, Myron's father strapped a beautiful gold watch on his son's wrist. The next day after school, Vinnie was full of admiration for the watch, while Myron was consumed with envy after one glance at the pistol. So the two friends decided to trade gifts.

That night when Vinnie checked to see whether it

was dinnertime, his father asked, "Where'd you get thatta watch?" And on hearing the story, he exploded. "Whatsa matter wid' yous? Here I am t'inkin' you gotta some brains in you head."

Vinnie looked frankly confused, so his father explained that some day Vinnie would probably get married. "An' somma day," he went on, "you's gonna find her in bed wit' another guy. An' whatta you gonna do then—look atta you watch and say, 'How long you gonna be?'"

□ □ □

Two Swedish sailors disembark in a sleazy little seaport and head for the nearest bar. Each orders a whisky, downs it in a gulp, orders another, downs it, and in short order puts away a third, fourth, and fifth drink. At this point Olaf orders yet another round, turns to his companion, and says, "*Sköl!*"

"Hey," returns the other Swede belligerently, "did you come here to bullshit or did you come here to drink?"

□ □ □

Do you know why Irish dogs have snub noses?

From chasing parked cars.

□ □ □

How come Irish women don't give good head?

They can't get their lips past his ears.

□ □ □

Three addicts went into a favorite back alley to shoot up. The black addict sterilized his needle, swabbed it with alcohol, and shot up. Then he passed it to the Jewish addict, who sterilized, swabbed it with alcohol, and shot up. Then he passed it to the Polish addict, who stuck the needle right in his arm.

"Are you crazy, man?" screamed the first two. "Haven't you heard of AIDS? You could get sick, man, you could *die*."

"Don't be ridiculous," said the Pole in a lofty tone. "I'm wearing a condom."

□ □ □

How do Italians count to ten?

"One, two, three, another, another, another. . . ."

□ □ □

What do Japanese men do when they have erections?

They vote.

□ □ □

Hear about the new synagogue in Harlem?

It's called Temple Beth-You-Is-My-Woman-Now.

□ □ □

Three men were hired to dig a six-foot ditch for the sanitation department. Soon the Italian laborer turned to his Polish buddy, who was slaving and sweating along next to him, and asked, "Say, how come we're down here doing all the work and he's up there telling us what to do?" And he gestured at the third hired hand, an Irishman, who was standing atop the pile of dirt.

"Got me," said the Pole. "Why don't you go ask him?" So the Italian climbed out of the ditch and posed the question.

"Let me illustrate why I'm up here and you're down there," suggested the Irishman, placing his hand against a tree. "Hit my hand as hard as you can with your shovel."

The Italian happily obeyed, but the Irishman pulled his hand away at the last moment. His hands aching and stinging from the force of the blow, the Italian was content to climb back down into the ditch.

"So how come we're down here and he's up there?" asked his buddy after a few minutes had passed in silence.

The Italian thought and thought, looking all around. Finally he moved his hand up in front of his face and said, "Hit my hand as hard as you can with your shovel."

□ □ □

How can you spot the Jewish Ethiopian?

He's the one with the Rolex around his waist.

□ □ □

What do you call hemorrhoids on an Eskimo?

Polaroids.

□ □ □

Three sailors, an Irishman, an Italian, and a black, were stranded in a life raft with the captain after their ship sank in a typhoon. After going through the emergency rations, the captain gravely announced that there was only enough food for three people. "One of you will have to swim for it, I'm afraid," he said, averting his eyes from the sharks circling the raft, "but to make it fair and square I'm going to ask each of you a question. If you answer correctly, you stay; if you blow it, out you go."

The three sailors nodded their agreement, and the captain turned to the Irishman. "What was the famous ship that was sunk by an iceberg?"

"The *Titanic*," answered the Irishman with a sigh of relief.

"How many people were killed?"

"Three thousand, four hundred and seventy," blurted the Italian, mopping the nervous sweat off his brow.

"Correct," noted the captain, turning to the black sailor. "Name them."

□ □ □

When Dino ran into Tony at the corner one night, he asked, "Yo, where you going?"

"I'm-a going to night school. You t'ink I wanna be stupid like you?"

"That so?" retorted Dino, thoroughly pissed off. "So whaddaya learn in school, anyway?"

"You know who Georgio Washing Machine was?" inquired Tony.

"No, who?"

"He was the first Presidente. How about Abraham Linguine, you heard-a him?"

"Nope," admitted Dino.

"Boy, are you stupid," sneered Tony. "He was the president who freed all the eggplants."

Embarrassed and furious, Dino retorted, "So, if you're so smart, who's-a Luigi Gondrevorta?"

Tony scratched his head. "We haven't gotten to him yet," he admitted. "Who's he?"

Dino roared with laughter. "You pretty stupid yourself. He's-a the guy been makin' love to your wife while you're at night school!"

□ □ □

Why do Mexicans drive low-riders?

So they can cruise and pick lettuce at the same time.

□ □ □

What do you get when you cross a Hungarian and an Italian?

A guy who makes you an offer you can't understand.

□ □ □

An Irishman, an Italian, and a Pole were sitting at a bar. Ordering a drink, the Irishman said, "I hate this place. I know a place on State Street where I can get every third drink free."

"That's nothing," returned the Italian. "I know a joint over on the west side where every other drink is free."

"Oh, yeah?" countered the Pole. "Well, I know a place on the south side where every drink is free, and at the end of the night you can get laid in the parking lot!"

"No kidding?" asked his companions. "That sounds great—where'd you hear about it?"

"From my wife," the Pole told them proudly.

□ □ □

And how can you spot a Puerto Rican intellectual?

He's the one who can read without moving his lips.

□ □ □

What do you call someone who's half Jewish and half black?

A Hebro.

□ □ □

An Irishman got engaged to a lovely Lithuanian girl, and when they went in for their blood tests it quickly became apparent to the doctor that the husband-to-be had no idea what sexual intercourse consisted of. Taking pity on the bride, Dr. Jones explained about the birds and the bees and the coconut trees, but the vague smile on the young man's face was unconvincing. The doctor's second attempt to explain the ritual of the wedding night left the Irishman smiling and nodding but clearly baffled. So the good doctor gave it one more try, to no avail.

Thoroughly frustrated, the doctor instructed the

young woman to undress and to lie down upon the examination table. She obeyed happily enough, and Dr. Jones, a humanitarian through and through, proceeded to demonstrate for the Irishman. For forty minutes he demonstrated. Finally, sweaty and exhausted, he hauled himself up on his elbows, turned to the fiancé, and said, "Now do you understand what I've been trying to tell you?"

At last a glimmer of comprehension came into the Irishman's blue eyes. "I've got it now, Doc," he cried happily.

"Good, good," said the doctor in relief, getting down from the table and pulling up his pants. "Do you have any further questions?"

"Just one," admitted the young man.

"Yes?" asked the doctor testily.

"All I need to know, Dr. Jones, is how often do I have to bring her in?"

□ □ □

When does a Mexican become a Spaniard?

When he marries into your family.

□ □ □

How many Ukrainians does it take to screw in a light bulb?

They don't need to; they glow in the dark.

□ □ □

A Russian, a Jamaican, an American, and a Mexican were on a rafting expedition together. In mid-river, the Russian pulled out a HUGE bottle of Stolichnaya, took a swig, and threw it overboard.

"Hey, what the hell'd you do that for?" blurted the American.

"We have so much vodka in Soviet Union that we can afford to waste it," explained the Russian cheerfully.

A few miles downstream the Jamaican took out a HUGE bag full of marijuana, rolled a giant joint, took a few puffs, and tossed it overboard.

"Jesus, that stuff's expensive," bellowed the American. "What'd you do that for?"

"In Jamaica, weed grows everywhere, mon," said the Jamaican with a grin. "We can afford to waste it."

Thinking hard, the American settled back into his seat. A few miles downriver he stood up with a smile and threw the Mexican overboard.

□ □ □

What do you get when you cross a black with a Japanese?

Someone who on December seventh has an uncontrollable urge to attack Pearl Bailey.

□ □ □

What's the ultimate in courage?

Letting an Ethiopian prostitute give you a blow job.

□ □ □

Miss DeAngelo was a none-too-bright Italian girl who had moved to Hollywood with dreams of becoming a star. She didn't find fame or glory, but she did encounter plenty of men willing to enjoy her plentiful charms, and eventually she found herself named in a divorce case.

When it was her turn on the stand, the prosecutor came forward. "Miss DeAngelo, the wife of the defendant has identified you as the 'other woman' in her husband's life. Now, do you admit that you went to the PriceRite Motel with this Mr. Evans?"

"Well, yes," acknowledged Miss DeAngelo with a sniff, "but I couldn't help it."

"Couldn't help it?" asked the lawyer derisively. "How's that?"

"Mr. Evans deceived me."

"Exactly what do you mean?"

"See, when we signed in," she explained, "he told the motel clerk I was his wife."

□ □ □

Heard about the black and the Mexican who opened up a restaurant?

It's called Nacho Mama.

□ □ □

Seen the Canadian bumper sticker?

It says, "I'd Rather Be Driving."

□ □ □

Why do Canadians like to do it doggie style?

So they can both keep watching the hockey game.

□ □ □

When Liam decided it was time for his friend Brendan to part with his virginity, he accompanied him to the local whorehouse and explained Brendan's condition to the madam. "Don't worry, my boy, we'll get a nice lass to take care of ye," she promised. "You just do your part and make sure ye wear one of these." And the madam took a condom out of her drawer and rolled it down over her thumb by way of instruction.

Brendan parted eagerly with his money and bounded up the stairs to Room Twelve, where a cheerful farm girl soon showed him the ropes. After he came, a frown passed over her face. "The rubber must have torn," she muttered. "I'm wet as the sea inside."

"Oh, no, it didn't, miss," Brendan cheerfully reassured her, holding up his thumb as evidence. "It's good as new."

□ □ □

How many U.S. Marines does it take to screw in a light bulb?

Fifty. One to screw it in and the other forty-nine to guard him.

□ □ □

How many Jews does it take to screw in a light bulb?

Three. One to call the cleaning lady, and the other two to feel guilty about having to call the cleaning lady.

□ □ □

And how many Teamsters does it take to change a light bulb?

Ten. You gotta PROBLEM with that?

□ □ □

Two white guys and a Puerto Rican found themselves up on the roof of the apartment building on a hot summer day. "Man, you should check this out," said one of them to the Puerto Rican, stepping up onto the parapet. "The wind really whips off the river around this building. Look." And he jumped off into space, plummeting for a few stories, then catching an updraft and floating gracefully to the sidewalk below like an autumn leaf.

Watching the maneuver in astonishment, the Puerto Rican guy gasped in admiration. Then, crossing himself, he took a flying leap off the building, only to splatter onto the street a few seconds later.

Surveying the gruesome spectacle, the other white guy ruefully shook his head. "What a racist asshole," he murmured. "That Clark Kent just can't stand Puerto Ricans."

□ □ □

The bitter Anatolian winter was almost over when one Armenian shepherd turned to the other and confessed that he could hardly wait until it was time to shear their flocks.

The other shepherd nodded, rubbing his hands together in anticipation. "It's great selling the wool in the market and spending some of the money on raki and women, eh?"

"That's not it," said his companion. "I just can't wait to see them naked."

□ □ □

Did you hear about the hillbilly who passed away and left his estate in trust for his bereaved widow?

She can't touch it till she's fourteen.

□ □ □

How many Irishmen does it take to change a light bulb?

Two. One to hold the bulb and the other to drink until the room spins.

□ □ □

How do you sink an Irish submarine?

Knock on the door.

□ □ □

The Ecuadorian Captain had grown increasingly anxious over rumors of an impending air strike from neighboring Peru. "Pedro," he ordered his aide-de-camp, "I want you to climb that mountain and report any signs of Peruvian military activity."

"*Sí, Capitano,*" replied Pedro. He trudged up the mountain, and as soon as he crossed the ridge he saw a squadron of planes heading their way. "There are many planes coming, *Capitano*," he promptly radioed back.

"Friends or enemies?" the Captain demanded urgently.

Pedro again lifted his binoculars to the sky. "They're flying very close together, *Capitano*," he replied. "I think they must be friends."

Polish

What does it say on the top of a Polish ladder?
"STOP!"

□ □ □

A carload of Polish friends came across the scene of an accident. "Oh, my God," gasped the driver, pulling over for a closer look at the crumpled sedan, "that looks like Joe's car." So they all piled out and walked closer.

"Look," said the second, "that's Joe's arm—I'd know that watch anywhere."

"I'm sure that's Joe's leg," said the third, pointing to where one limb had rolled up against the curb.

"And look—that's definitely Joe's head," shouted the fourth, running after an object rolling slowly down the street. "Joe, Joe," he cried, picking it up, "are you all right?"

□ □ □

Three high-school pals were walking down the boardwalk when they came across a gorgeous girl in a string bikini. Two of the guys let out wolf whistles and stared their eyes out, but the third, who happened to be Polish, took to his heels in the opposite direction.

A few days later all three were walking down the boardwalk again and came across the same girl, this time wearing nothing but the bikini bottom. And again, two of the guys went ape while the Polish fellow ran for his life.

So when the guys saw the girl a third time—this time she was stark naked—two of them grabbed the Pole before he could get away. Shaking him by the shoulders, they shouted, "Why're you running away from a gorgeous sight like that, you jerk?"

Trembling, the Pole blurted, "See, it's like this: My mother told me if I ever looked at a naked woman I'd turn into stone . . . and I felt something getting hard."

□ □ □

Early one morning, while his son was getting ready for his first day of school, a Polish father took him aside and proceeded to instruct him on the appropriate way to urinate. "Okay, son: one, unzip your pants. Two, take out your penis. Three, pull back the foreskin. Four, pee into the urinal. Five, shake your penis off. Six, push back your foreskin. And finally, replace your penis and zip your fly back up."

Later that day, the father received a call from his son's teacher. "What seems to be the problem?" he asked.

"Well," the teacher said, somewhat perplexed, "it appears that your son doesn't want to leave the bathroom."

"Oh, really? What's he doing in there?"

"We're not sure. He just keeps repeating, 'Three-six, Three-six.'"

□ □ □

Jerzy and Latvia were bored one day and decided to go to the zoo and taunt the gorillas. As they made faces at the apes, they didn't notice that one of the animals was getting quite turned on by Latvia's tits. All of a sudden, the ape reached through the bars, grabbed ahold of Latvia's blouse, and pulled her into his cage.

"What should I do!?" she screamed at Jerzy as the gorilla tore her skirt off and started to sexually assault her.

"I dunno. Tell him what you tell me all the time, that you have a headache."

□ □ □

What does a Polish girl get on her wedding night that's long and hard?

A new last name.

□ □ □

Why did the Pole drive around the block fifty-seven times?

His turn signal was stuck.

□ □ □

How about the one who got his dick stuck in the battery?

He was told he had to jump it in order to get his car started.

□ □ □

Two Poles were watching the game on TV when a commercial for Tucks Hemorrhoidal Medicated Pads came on, showing a hot match being extinguished in a moist pad. "Tucks Medicated Pads relieve the burning and itching of hemorrhoidal tissue," said the soothing voice-over.

"I've got to buy myself some of those," said the first Pole, confiding that his hemorrhoids had really been bothering him.

"Well, what do you expect," cried his buddy, "when you keep sticking lit matches up your ass!"

□ □ □

Hear about the Polish kid whose teacher told him to write a 100-word essay on what he did during summer vacation?

He wrote "Not much" fifty times.

□ □ □

Two little Polish girls were walking down the block to school and one said to the other, "Hey, know what I found on the patio the other day? A contraceptive."

"Oh, yeah?" said her friend. "What's a patio?"

□ □ □

When Mr. Petrowski realized he was having trouble reading road signs, he knew it was time to visit the eye doctor and get his first pair of glasses. Seating him in front of the eye chart, the opthamologist instructed his patient to cover one eye with his hand. But despite the doctor's repeated instructions, Mr. Petrowski seemed incapable of anything other than a saluting motion.

Finally the opthamologist lost all patience. Fashioning a mask out of a brown paper bag and cutting out a hole for one eye, he put it over the man's head. "How does that feel, Mr. Petrowski?" he asked.

After a little pause, Petrowski answered, "The fit is fine, Doctor, but I confess I was hoping for something a little more stylish. Maybe something in a tortoiseshell frame?"

□ □ □

What were Jesus' last instructions to the Polish people?

"Play dumb till I get back."

□ □ □

The basketball coach stormed into the university president's office and demanded a raise right then and there.

"Jesus Christ, man," protested President Kubritski. "You already make more than the entire English department!"

"Yeah, maybe so, but you don't know what I have to put up with," the coach blustered. "Look." He went out into the hall and grabbed a jock who was jogging down the hallway. "Run over to my office and see if I'm there," he ordered.

Twenty minutes later the jock returned, sweaty and out of breath. "You're not there, sir," he reported.

"Oh, I see what you mean," conceded President Kubritski, scratching his head. "I would have phoned."

□ □ □

How does a Pole rob a drive-in window at the bank?

He puts his gun in the little basket along with a note that says, "This is a stickup."

□ □ □

How come the Pole returned his necktie?

It was too tight.

□ □ □

Why do Polish names end in "ski"?

They don't know how to spell "toboggan."

□ □ □

A middle-aged man walked into a store, went up to the counter, and said, "I'd like to order a Polish dog."

Looking up from his ledger, the owner asked, "Are you Polish, by any chance?"

"And just why is that your concern?" retorted the would-be customer. "If I ordered French fries, would you ask me if I were French? I think not. And if I wanted Swiss cheese on my hamburger, would you assume I'm from Switzerland? I doubt it. So why, then, do you ask me if I'm Polish when I order a Polish dog?"

"Because," explained the owner, "this is a florist."

□ □ □

How many Poles does it take to rape a girl?

Four. Three to hold her down, and one to read the instructions.

□ □ □

Did you hear about the Polish woman who bought an exercise bike and died the very same day?

She tried to ride it home.

□ □ □

Why do Poles have broad shoulders and broad heads?

Because when you ask them a question [shrug your shoulders] they shrug their shoulders, and when you tell them the answer [slap the top of your head] they slap the top of their heads and say, "Christ, why didn't I think of that?"

□ □ □

Did you hear about the first Polish space mission? The launch went off without a hitch, they reached orbit, and the first astronaut left the capsule to walk in space. When he knocked on the door to be let back in in, the other astronaut asked, "Who's there?"

□ □ □

Judge: "The charge is the theft of sixteen turnips. Are you the defendant?"

Polish Defendant: "No, sir. I'm the guy who stole the turnips."

□ □ □

Why did the Pole ask everyone to save their burned-out light bulbs?

He needed them for the darkroom he was building.

□ □ □

Did you hear about the Pole who went ice fishing and brought home 100 pounds of ice?

His wife drowned trying to cook it.

□ □ □

How about the adventurous Pole who got a zebra for a pet?

He named it Spot.

□ □ □

Can you figure out why Poland's going to declare war on the United States in about fifteen years?

That's when they're going to start understanding these jokes.

Black

We all know of the scholarship fund started by Ric[h] Pryor and Michael Jackson called the Ignited Negro [Col]lege Fund. . . .

But did you know they were both awarded hono[rary] degrees as Extinguished Alumni?

□ □ □

What's the black version of a fortune cookie?

A piece of cornbread with a food stamp in the [mid]dle.

□ □ □

A bus driver in Tuscaloosa constantly had to put up [with] fights between his black passengers and his white on[es as] to who had the right to sit where. Finally he pulle[d the] bus over, made everyone get off, and lectured t[hem] sternly. "From now on, there ain't gonna be no [more] fightin' 'bout who's better, black or white. From no[w on] you're all blue."

The passengers looked each other over sheepishl[y and] repeated, "We're all blue. Right on—we're all the sa[me]."

"Good," said the driver. "Now, back on the b[us]: sky blue people in front, navy blue people in back.[”]

□ □ □

What do you call a white man surrounded by three blacks?

Victim.

□ □ □

What do you call a white man surrounded by five blacks?

Coach.

□ □ □

What do you call a white man surrounded by ten blacks?

Quarterback.

□ □ □

And what do you call a white man surrounded by three hundred blacks?

Warden.

□ □ □

A little black kid decided to enter a cock contest sponsored by a local bar. When he walked in the door that night carrying a huge trophy, his mother asked how he had won it.

"I entered this contest to see who had the biggest cock, Ma," explained the kid. "The first white guy pulled out a cock that measured ten inches. The second white guy pulled one out that measured fifteen inches. Then it was my—"

The boy's mother interrupted him with a scream of alarm. "My God, Joey, you didn't pull that whole thing out, now did you?"

"Hell, no, Ma," replied the eight-year-old bashfully, "just enough to win."

□ □ □

What did George Washington and Thomas Jefferson have in common?

They were the last white people to have those names.

□ □ □

Heard about the new toy store in Harlem?

It's called "We Be Toys."

□ □ □

Did you hear about the sequel to *Shogun* with an all-black cast?

It's going to be called *Shonuff*.

□ □ □

To keeps his costs down, Farmer Brown bought some robots to work his fields. Profits were increasing nicely when he received a visit from a representative of the State Highway Commission. Apparently the sunlight reflecting off the robots was disturbing westbound motorists on the nearby interstate.

"No problem," said Farmer Brown agreeably, and overnight he painted all the robots black.

The next morning only two showed up for work.

□ □ □

What do you call a rich black man in Bangkok?

A Tycoon.

□ □ □

How do you make a black person nervous?

Take him to an auction.

□ □ □

Did you hear about Evel Knievel's cousin, Ku Klux Knievel?

He tried to jump over seventeen blacks—with a steamroller.

□ □ □

The top brass at NASA was getting flak about never having sent a black man to the moon, so the next moon shot went up with a black astronaut aboard. The only hitch was that the decision had been so sudden that the fellow hadn't even been briefed. His only instructions were to strap himself in, wait till he reached an altitude of five miles, and remove his helmet. The craft was on complete automatic pilot, so Mission Control wasn't too worried.

On the way up the astronaut had plenty of time to reflect on his role as the token black, and on what racist assholes ran NASA. If only he could prove it, could find some hard evidence. As he was musing, the spacecraft reached the designated altitude, and as the astronaut removed his helmet he was startled to hear a noise from elsewhere on the ship. Investigating, he was shocked to come across another passenger, a chimpanzee in full astronaut garb! The monkey, too, had just removed his helmet, but it seemed to be studying a computer terminal in front of its seat.

"I don't have a terminal," the astronaut thought to himself. "What's going on here?" Looking over the chimp's shoulders, he saw that the screen contained a list of operating instructions for the mission's data-gathering operations. His worst fears were confirmed when, in shock, he read the last item on the list:

1800 HOURS—FEED THE ASTRONAUT.

□ □ □

What do seven-foot black basketball players do in the off-season?

Go to the movies and sit in front of you!

□ □ □

What do blacks and sperm have in common?

Only one in two million does any real work.

□ □ □

Trying desperately to establish the reliability and good character of his witness, the public defender asked, "Johnson, tell us, is your widowed mother dependent on you?"

"She sure is," replied Johnson with a big smile. "Why, if I didn't go pick up the washing and bring it home for her to do, truth is, the old lady'd starve to death."

□ □ □

Why was the black acquitted of rape on grounds of temporary insanity?

Because when he got an erection, there was no blood left to flow to his brain.

□ □ □

Miss Struthers asked her fifth-graders to name the most important invention in the history of the world. "Yes, Luanne," she began, pointing at a little girl in the front row.

"The plane, Miss Struthers," she replied. "Now people can travel really far, really easily and fast."

"Yes, Billy?" The teacher nodded at a little boy, who suggested the telephone. "It makes it so people from all over the world can talk to each other."

"Very good, Billy."

"Miss Struthers, I know, I know!" The teacher turned in some surprise to a little black kid in the back row who was waving his arm and jumping up and down in his seat.

"Yes, Marcus? Go ahead."

"It's the thermos, Miss Struthers. It keeps hot things hot and cold things cold—and *how* do it know?"

□ □ □

The poor black boy from Macon, Georgia, felt a wave of panic come over him as he surveyed the all-white jury in the New Hampshire courthouse. Positive he'd never beat the murder rap, he managed to get hold of one of the kindlier-looking jurors, and bribe her with his life savings to go for a manslaughter verdict.

Sure enough, at the close of the trial the jury declared him guilty of manslaughter. Tears of gratitude welling up in his eyes, the young man had a moment with the juror before being led off to prison. "Thank you, thank you—how'd you do it?"

"It wasn't easy," she admitted. "They all wanted to acquit you."

□ □ □

Did you hear about the ad for BMWs in *Ebony?*

It says, "You've got the radio—now get the car."

□ □ □

What do steroids and the South African government have in common?

They both make blacks run faster.

Jewish

How does a JAP do it doggie-style?

The husband gets on all fours and she rolls over and plays dead.

□ □ □

What's the difference between a JAP and taxes?

Taxes suck.

□ □ □

One Sunday, an old Jewish man walked into a Catholic Church and sat down in a confessional.

"Forgive me, Father, for I have sinned," he said humbly. "Yesterday afternoon a beautiful girl with gigantic breasts and a cute little tush valked into my delicatessen and started making nice to me. Vell, what can I tell you, I closed the store and for the next six hours I fucked her. I vas like a crazy man or something."

"Excuse me, Mr. Epstein," interrupted a perplexed priest. "but you're Jewish. Why are you telling me?"

"Telling *you?*" yelled old Epstein. "I'm telling everyone!"

□ □ □

Did you hear about the new Israeli Army doll for girls?

It's called G.I. JAP.

□ □ □

Why was the JAP snorting Nutra-Sweet?
She thought it was Diet Coke.

□ □ □

What do you call a Japanese JAP?
An Orienta.

□ □ □

An extremely pale, slight man wearing dark glasses stood out from the usual crowd by a Miami Beach pool. Mrs. Kravitz took an immediate interest in the newcomer. Settling herself next to his deck chair, she introduced herself and asked, "Why so pale?"

"Leave me alone, lady," grunted the man, "I just got outta jail."

"Oh, I see," said Mrs. Kravitz, pursing her lips. "How long for?"

"Five years."

"That's terrible," she clucked. "For what?"

"Embezzlement."

"Ooh." Mrs. Kravitz nodded knowledgeably.

"And then five years for armed robbery," said the man in a sudden burst of talkativeness, "and then another lousy ten."

"And what was that for?"

"I killed my wife."

A big smile coming over her face, Mrs. Kravitz sat bolt upright. "Myrna," she screeched across the pool to her friend, "he's *single!*"

□ □ □

Did you hear about the Jewish porn movie?
It's called *Debbie Does Bubkis*.

□ □ □

What's the difference between an Israelite and an Israeli?
About thirty calories.

□ □ □

What's "perfect sex" to a JAP?
Simultaneous headaches.

□ □ □

A devout Jew, Mrs. Feinstein offered up her prayers each week in temple. One week she prayed especially fervently. "Lord, I have always been a good Jew, and I've had a good life. I only have one complaint: I'm poor. Please, Lord, let me win the lottery."

The next week, Mrs. Feinstein was a little more strident. "Lord," she prayed, "have I ever missed a High Holy Day? Not fasted on Yom Kippur? Why must I go to my grave a pauper? One lottery win is all I'm asking you for."

The third week Mrs. Feinstein made no bones about her displeasure. "A faithful Jew such as myself, Lord, always observant, always dutiful, asks for one little favor, and what do I get. . . ?"

A glowing, white-bearded figure stepped down from the heavens and into the temple. "Now, Mrs. Feinstein," boomed God, "don't you think you could at least meet me halfway, and buy a ticket?"

□ □ □

One day, a JAP goes home and tells her mother that she's been raped by a large black man.

"Well, hurry, go into the kitchen, cut up a lemon and suck on it," her mother instructed.

"Will that keep me from getting pregnant?" the JAP asked.

"No," the mother snapped, "but it'll wipe that stupid grin off your face."

□ □ □

Milton came into his JAP wife's room one day. "If I were, say, disfigured, would you still love me?" he asked her.

"Darling, I'll always love you," she said calmly, filing her nails.

"How about if I became impotent, couldn't make love to you any more?" he asked anxiously.

"Don't worry, darling, I'll always love you," she told him, buffing her nails.

"Well, how about if I lost my job as vice president?" Milton went on. "If I weren't pulling in six figures any more? Would you still love me then?"

The JAP looked over at her husband's worried face. "Milton, I'll always love you," she reassured him, "but most of all, I'll really miss you."

□ □ □

What's the definition of a Jewish nymphomaniac?

One that'll have sex even when she's just had her hair done.

□ □ □

An old Jew was retiring from the string and twine business. "Herschel," he implored his best friend, "I got one last load of string. Buy me out so I can retire with an empty shop and a clear heart."

Herschel had no interest in purchasing a load of string but his old friend's impassioned pleading eventually wore him down. "Myron, all right, all right," he finally conceded. "I'll buy some of your string—enough to reach from the tip of your nose to the tip of your dick."

To Herschel's surprise, his friend embraced him

warmly and left without another word. He was even more surprised when a truck arrived the next morning loaded with a massive roll of string. "Myron, what is this?!" he screamed at his friend over the phone.

"My nose is in Palm Beach," explained Myron happily, "but the tip of my dick is buried somewhere outside Minsk."

□ □ □

How can you spot a disadvantaged Jewish teenager?

He's driving a domestic car.

□ □ □

How can you tell the mother-in-law at a Jewish wedding?

She's the one on her hands and knees, picking up the rice.

□ □ □

Why aren't Jewish mothers attacked by sharks?

Professional courtesy.

□ □ □

Levin was a notorious tightwad, and alleviated his few twinges of conscience by giving a quarter to the miserable-looking woman who sold bagels from a pushcart on the corner by his office. He never bought a bagel, having already breakfasted, but he always put a quarter into her grimy palm and felt himself a virtuous man.

This went on for months, until one day the bagel-seller tugged at his immaculate cuff. "Mister, Mister, I gotta tell ya somethin'."

"Ah," acknowledged Levin with a gracious smile, "I suppose you wish to know why I give you a quarter every day but never take the bagel?"

"Nah, that's yer business," she snorted. "My business is tellin' ya the price's gone up to thirty-five cents."

□ □ □

What did the Jewish mother bank teller say to her customers?

"You never write, you never call, you only visit when you need money."

□ □ □

When Selma answered her phone, it happened to be an obscene phone call. The man on the other end began describing in detail all the kinky, perverted sexual acts he wanted to engage in with her.

"Now hang on, wait just a minute," Selma interrupted. "All this you know from me just saying hello?"

□ □ □

What did the Jewish mother ask her daughter when she learned she'd had an affair?

"Who catered it?"

Wasp

Why don't WASP girls like gang bangs?
For one thing, the sex is icky; and then there're all those thank-you notes.

□ □ □

What's a WASP's idea of mass transit?
The ferry to Martha's Vineyard.

□ □ □

What do you call a skinny Protestant?
A Wisp.

□ □ □

The Driscolls were driving home from the Forbes's cocktail party when Mindy broke the stony silence. "Why on earth did you tell Chip you married me because I was such a terrific cook? You know I can't boil water, for God's sake."

"Because I had to say *something*," he retorted.

□ □ □

After a very sheltered childhood, it was mildly surprising that Hackley managed to get a decent job, persuade a nice girl to marry him, and father a son and heir. "Now, darling," coached his wife, "don't forget to drop by St. Thomas's and ask the Rector to arrange for little Hackley's christening."

"Are you sure about that?" the proud father asked, looking down at the tiny squalling bundle. "He seems awfully small to have a bottle smashed over his head."

□ □ □

Why don't WASPs approve of artificial insemination?

They don't approve of using someone else's left-overs.

□ □ □

What do you get when you cross a WASP and a Mexican?

A migrant stockbroker.

□ □ □

Why do WASPs fly so much?

For the food.

□ □ □

"We have a new baby at our house," reported Spencer to Chandler at tumbling class.

"Neat! Is it a boy or a girl?"

"I don't know," admitted Spencer. "They haven't dressed it yet."

□ □ □

Lives of considerable privilege had accustomed Chauncey and Skiff to getting their own way, and this attitude accompanied them on a trip to Europe following their graduation from Princeton. After lunch in a little brasserie on the Rive Gauche, Chauncey snapped his fingers for *l'addition*, and when Skiff got back from the men's room, Chauncey was scowling at the bill and yelling at the cowering waitress. "I think the waitress is shortchanging me," he explained, "but I can't understand a damn thing she says. Can you believe she can't speak English? *You* took French at Andover, Skiff—help me out, won't you?"

Skiff strode over to confront the waitress. "*Parlez-vous Français, mademoiselle?*" he asked.

"*Oui, oui, monsieur,*" she answered in evident relief.

"Well, then," he demanded, "why the hell won't you give my pal here the right change?"

□ □ □

"On my side of the family, we can trace our lineage back to the Tudor kings," Cholmondeley boasted to Evans in the steam room after a grueling game of squash.

"No kidding?" said Evans drily. "And I suppose your folks were right there on the bow of the Mayflower too?"

"Of course not," sniffed Cholmondeley. "We always had our own boats."

□ □ □

Young Mrs. Townsend wanted very much to participate in the correct charities, and when the annual Junior League Easter Charity Ball came around, she volunteered to head the committee. It took a lot of organizing, but the party went off without a hitch, and she dined and danced into the wee hours.

When the festivities ended, she was dismayed to observe a bag lady bundled on the sidewalk next to her Saab Turbo. Hearing the rustle of Mrs. Townsend's taffeta skirts, the old woman extended a grimy palm and asked the socialite if she could spare any change.

"Oooh," gasped Mrs. Townsend, "the nerve. And after I spend all night slaving to help people like you! Aren't you *ever* satisfied?"

□ □ □

Definition of a WASP:

Someone who thinks Taco Bell is the Mexican phone company.

□ □ □

During brunch at the yacht club, R. Chip Frothingham III took the family doctor aside and confided that he and his wife were having difficulty conceiving.

"I'm not a fertility expert, Chip, but maybe I can help," Dr. Spicer offered kindly. "What position are you in when you ejaculate?"

"Uh . . . what do you mean by ejaculation, Doctor?"

"When you climax?"

The young man still looked blank, so the doctor tried again. "When you come, Chip. Don't you come?"

Chip's face suddenly brightened. "Oh, do you mean that sticky white stuff, Dr. Spicer? Buffy thinks it's yucky, so I make sure to shoot it into the sink before getting into bed."

□ □ □

Why do WASPs play golf?

It's the only chance they get to dress up like black people.

Handicapped

A door-to-door vacuum cleaner salesman was quite taken aback when a truly horrible-looking little boy, his face mangled and his body twisted, answered the doorbell. Appalled by his deformities, the salesman still managed to speak up. "Good morning, young man, is your mom at home? I'd like to sell her a vacuum cleaner."

"She's in an institution," mumbled the lad, whose cleft palate kept him from speaking very clearly.

"I see," said the salesman, warming to his pitch. "Can I speak to your dad, then?"

"Nope. He's in an institution too."

"So how about I talk to your older brother, and maybe leave my calling card?" the salesman suggested hopefully.

"He's at Harvard," said the little boy patiently.

"Now, wait a minute," said the salesman after thinking this over. "Your mom and dad are both in institutions and—no offense—you don't look so hot yourself, but your brother's at *Harvard*? What's he doing there?"

"He's in a jar."

□ □ □

How do you make a Venetian blind?

Poke him in the eye.

□ □ □

Mrs. Jones began to get nervous when dark fell and her husband hadn't returned from his regular Saturday golf game. Dinnertime came and went and she became more and more anxious, so when she heard his car pull in, she rushed out to the driveway. "Where've you been? I've been worried sick!" she exclaimed.

"Harry had a heart attack on the third hole," her husband explained.

"Oh, no! That's terrible."

"You're telling me," moaned her husband. "All day long it was hit the ball, drag Harry, hit the ball, drag Harry . . . ."

□ □ □

Graffiti in the men's room:

"DYSLEXICS, UNTIE!"

□ □ □

Which doesn't fit with the rest: AIDS, herpes, gonorrhea, condominiums?

Gonorrhea. You can get rid of it.

□ □ □

What do you call a hippy with no legs?

A veteran.

□ □ □

A man came into the psychiatrist's office, reclined on the couch, and told the doctor he needed help ridding his mind of an obsession. "All I can think of, day and night, is making love to a horse. It's driving me nuts."

"I see," said the shrink, rubbing his goatee. "Now would that be to a stallion or to a mare?"

"A mare, of course," retorted the patient, pulling

himself upright indignantly. "What do you think I am, a pervert or something?"

□ □ □

Why don't midgets use Tampax?
They trip on the strings.

□ □ □

Among many other attractions, the traveling circus featured Wanda the Wondrous, a faith healer who claimed the ability to heal any malady, slight or serious, real or imagined. She usually drew a big crowd, from which she would select a few people on whom to practice her healing skills. Among the unfortunates one Friday night were Cecily Sussman, on crutches due to a congenitally malformed spine, and Irving Bland, who had suffered from a terrible lisp all his life. "Cecily and Irving," asked Wanda, "do you wish to be healed?"

"Yeth, ma'am," said Irving, and Cecily nodded vigorously.

Wanda motioned them behind a purple velvet curtain and proceeded to chant and pray, grinding powders together and swaying before the audience. Finally she intoned, "Cecily, throw out your left crutch."

A crutch came sailing over the curtain.

"Cecily, throw out your right crutch."

A second crutch clattered on the floor at the healer's feet.

"Now, Irving," asked Wanda solemnly, "say something to the people."

Irving's voice rang out clearly from behind the purple curtain. "Thethily Thuthman jutht fell on her ath."

□ □ □

What do you call a one-legged ballerina's costume?
A one-one.

□ □ □

Seen the new medic-alert tags for epileptics?
They say, "I am not break dancing."

□ □ □

"Yeah, Doc, what's the news?" answered Fred when his doctor called with his test results.

"I have some bad news and some really bad news," admitted the doctor. "The bad news is that you only have twenty-four hours to live."

"Oh, my God," gasped Fred, sinking to his knees. "What could be worse news than that?"

"I couldn't get hold of you yesterday."

□ □ □

Seen on a matchbook cover in Ohio:

ILLITERATE?
WRITE FOR FREE HELP

□ □ □

If a waitress with one leg is called Eileen—
and a Japanese waitress with one leg is called Irene—
where do they work?

At the I-Hop!

□ □ □

Aunt Jean was rattling along in her Oldsmobile when she got a flat tire. Being an independent sort, she jacked up the car and undid the nuts and bolts, but as she was pulling the tire off, she lost her balance and fell backward onto the hubcap holding the hardware. And it rolled right down into a storm sewer.

This entire incident occurred right outside the state insane asylum and happened to be observed by an inmate watching carefully through the bars. "Listen, lady," he called out, "just use one bolt from each of the other three tires. They'll be plenty strong enough to get you to the gas station."

"Quick thinking," said Aunt Jean admiringly. "Now, why on earth is a bright boy like you stuck in that place?"

"Lady, I'm here for being crazy, not stupid."

□ □ □

Why don't blind people skydive?

Because it scares the hell out of their seeing-eye dogs.

□ □ □

Heard about the new Cabbage Patch Doll with AIDS?

It comes with its own death certificate.

□ □ □

"Shep's a really nice guy, Barbara, and I'm sure you really love him, but how can you bear being married to a quadriplegic?" Cynthia marveled to her model girlfriend. "He can't even wiggle his little finger. And let's face it: With your face and your body, you could have picked just about any guy on the planet."

"You don't get it, Cyn," replied Barbara. "Who needs fingers? Shep's tongue is eight inches long."

"An eight-inch tongue?" Cynthia gasped.

"And that's not all," continued Barbara smugly. "He's learned to breathe through his ears."

□ □ □

How many paranoid schizophrenics does it take to screw in a light bulb?

Who wants to know?

□ □ □

What did one blind Pole keep asking the other blind Pole?

"Is your dick bigger than mine?"

□ □ □

Why is it a bad idea to date a woman with no hands?
You'll never know how she feels.

□ □ □

What song did the mermaid sing to the sailors?
"I can't give you anything but head, baby."

□ □ □

The middle-aged man walked into the bar with a shit-eating grin on his face and ordered a round for the house. "It's nice to see someone in such a good mood," commented the bartender. "Mind if I ask why?"

"This is the happiest day of my life—I'm finally taller than my brother Jim," explained the fellow, beaming from ear to ear.

The bartender studied his customer disbelievingly. "Are you trying to tell me that at your age you actually grew taller?"

"Of course not! See, Jim was in an accident on the Interstate yesterday," the fellow explained cheerfully, "and they had to amputate both his legs."

□ □ □

"Andrew, I'm really worried about Patty," confessed James to his best friend over the phone. "She wasn't home when I got here, she hasn't called, and it's after midnight. You know how depressed she's been since her mastectomy. . . . Think something could have happened to her?"

"Now try not to worry," his buddy said soothingly. "Maybe Patty went out for a drink. Maybe she's visiting a friend, know what I mean?"

James glanced at the bedside table and shook his head glumly. "I doubt it. She left her tits behind."

□ □ □

How did the sympathetic doctor treat the kleptomaniac?

He gave her something to take.

□ □ □

Heard about the new nonprofit institution called AMD?

It's "Mothers Against Dyslexia."

□ □ □

Mrs. Stone despaired of her humpbacked daughter's marital prospects, since several social seasons in Shaker Heights hadn't produced a single possibility. So she packed her off to Paris, where she hoped the family's considerable fortune would render Jill more attractive.

Sure enough, the girl soon made the acquaintance of a Frenchman from a noble if impoverished family, and when he proposed marriage, she was beside herself with joy. After the final fitting of her Dior wedding dress, Henri took Jill to meet his aged mother, whose consent was necessary. "Don't worry, *ma cherie*," he said sweetly, "your refined ways and quaint accent will positively charm *Maman*. Just one thing, though: You've got to straighten up."

□ □ □

When Robinson stretched out on the psychiatrist's couch, he was clearly in a bad state. "Doctor," he pleaded, voice quavering and hands twitching, "you've got to help me. I really think I'm losing my mind. I have no memory of what happened to me a year ago, nor even of a few weeks back. I can't even recall yesterday with any clarity. I can't cope with daily life—in fact, I think I'm going insane."

"Keep calm, Mr. Robinson," soothed the shrink. "I'm sure I'll be able to help you. Now tell me: How long have you had this problem?"

Robinson looked up blankly. "What problem?"

Leper

What happened when the leper's mom died?
He fell apart.

□ □ □

Why didn't the leper cross the road?
He didn't have the balls.

□ □ □

How do lepers commit suicide?
By giving head.

□ □ □

What happened to the leper when he visited Times Square?
Someone stole his kneecaps.

□ □ □

Why is this book off limits to lepers?
They might laugh their asses off.

□ □ □

What's the best thing about marrying a girl who has leprosy?
She can only give you lip once.

Helen Keller

What's Helen Keller's idea of oral sex?
A manicure.

□ □ □

How did Helen Keller pierce her ear?
Answering the stapler.

□ □ □

What did Helen Keller say when someone handed her a cheese grater?
"That's the most violent story I've ever read."

□ □ □

Did you hear about Helen Keller's speech impediment?
Calluses.

□ □ □

How come Helen Keller never changed her baby?
So she always knew where to find him.

□ □ □

What was the meanest present under the Keller Christmas tree?

Rubik's Cube.

□ □ □

Okay, but what was the second meanest?
A paint-by-number set.

□ □ □

And what was the meanest present Helen Keller ever gave away?
Her first paint-by-number picture.

□ □ □

How did Helen Keller discover masturbation?
Trying to read her own lips.

□ □ □

So why does she masturbate with just one hand?
So she can moan with the other.

Homosexual

A homosexual gets some suppositories from his doctor, but he doesn't know how to insert them up his own asshole.

"Before you get dressed in the morning," the doctor instructs, "stand on a mirror and bend over. You should have no problem."

Before getting dressed the next morning, the fag takes his mirror down off the wall and stands on it. Suddenly, he gets a terrific boner. Chuckling, the fag looks at his dick and murmurs, "It's just me, sweetie."

□ □ □

What's a Jewish mother's dilemma?

Having a gay son who's dating a doctor.

□ □ □

A car runs into the rear of the car in front waiting at a stoplight. A fag jumps out shrieking, "My car! Look what you did! I'm going to sue you for five thousand dollars!"

"Five thousand dollars?" yelled the other driver in amazement. "All I did was dent your bumper a bit. You can just kiss my ass!"

"Well, well," conceded the fag with a smile, "maybe we can settle out of court."

□ □ □

Two Polish gays enjoy a long night of wild anal and oral sex. As one of them is leaving the next morning, he puts out his hand to shake goodbye.

"What! Are you crazy?" admonished the other fag. "I heard you can get AIDS that way!"

□ □ □

A county sheriff picked up a fag from the big city after the residents of the sleepy little town complained that the homo was propositioning some of the local boys.

"Okay, you fruitcake," the sheriff said in disgust, "you got fifteen minutes to blow this town or I'll throw your queer ass in jail."

"Oh, my," cooed the fag, "I'd better get started. I *love* a challenge."

□ □ □

What's the gay scoutmaster's motto?

"Out of every young scout, a mature man will emerge."

□ □ □

What's the Phone Sex company's motto?

"Reach out and touch someone's."

□ □ □

A cab driver struck up a casual conversation with his passenger, who suddenly asked, "Say, if you woke up in the morning and found Vaseline on your asshole, would you tell anyone?"

"Gee . . ." answered the startled cabbie, "no, I don't think I would."

"Great!" said the passenger. "Would you go camping with me?"

□ □ □

What's the definition of a lesbian?

Just another damn woman trying to do a man's job.

□ □ □

A wino scraped together five dollars, bought and downed two bottles of Thunderbird, and passed out behind a hedge in a nearby park. Not long afterward a fag strolled by and noticed him. "That's appealing," he thought to himself, and he rolled the wino over and fucked him. It was such a pleasant experience that he tucked five dollars in the drunk's pocket and went on his way.

When the wino woke up he was amazed to find his pocket still had money in it. Hurrying over to the liquor store, he proceeded to spend it on wine and pass out in the same place, where the fag found him on his way out to lunch. Quite delighted, the fag had another go and tucked another five dollars in his pocket.

This time the wino could hardly believe his good fortune. Again he got drunk and passed out, and again he was found and screwed. Unable to believe *his* good fortune, the grateful fag tucked twenty dollars in the wino's pocket and went home.

When the wino came to, he pulled the twenty dollars out of his pocket. Clutching it tightly, he staggered to the liquor store and beckoned to the clerk. "Hey, buddy, get me some good wine off the shelf," he instructed the clerk, "cause this cheap stuff's killing my asshole."

□ □ □

What do you call three lesbians in bed together?

A ménage à twat.

□ □ □

What do Chinese homosexuals and black homosexuals have in common?

They both give bro jobs.

□ □ □

The English officer was not particularly pleased when he was assigned to a detachment of American soldiers in a NATO post, and his worst fears were confirmed when the American officer in charge came over and slapped him on the back. "Hey, there, Nigel," he boomed, "call me Biff."

"You're going to like our camp," the American went on heartily. "We don't just sit around watching the grass grow and waiting for orders, you know. Take Monday nights. On Mondays we all get drunk as skunks."

"Count me out," said the Englishman stiffly. "I don't drink."

"Hey, pal, that's okay," the American reassured him. "You'll have some fun on Tuesday nights when we all get wrecked on weed."

"I wouldn't think of it."

"Not to worry," the American officer went on, "because you'll love Wednesdays. That's when we bring the local chicks over and the real fun begins."

"I hate to disappoint you, old chap," said Nigel, "but I do not consort with cheap women."

"You don't?" The American was clearly puzzled. "Say, you aren't one of those queers, are you?"

"Certainly not!" retorted the Brit, highly insulted.

Biff whistled through his teeth. "Well, for sure you're not gonna like Thursday nights."

□ □ □

What's the hardest thing about having AIDS?

Trying to convince your parents you're Haitian.

□ □ □

What do you call hemorrhoids on a fag?
Speed bumps.

□ □ □

Over lunch in the hospital cafeteria, one doctor happened to mention to his colleague that he'd come across a nutritional breakthrough for his AIDS patients. "Pancakes," he explained cheerfully.

"Really?" commented his friend. "I wasn't aware that pancakes had any special nutritional value."

"They don't," replied the first doctor, "but they're so easy to slide under the door."

□ □ □

What do you call a Playboy bunny who's a lesbian?
Bitch.

□ □ □

How do you get hearing AIDS?
From listening to assholes.

□ □ □

Handsome Vinnie had a great vacation visiting the back room of every gay bar on Castro Street, but it left him somewhat the worse for wear. When he got home he called up a friend who practiced homeopathic medicine and complained that his rectum was terribly swollen and tender. The friend recommended making a poultice of herbal tea leaves and applying it to the area.

It did relieve the irritation a bit, but the next morning found Vinnie still in considerable discomfort, so he hobbled over to the office of a proctologist who served the gay community. In the examining room, the good-looking fellow bent over and spread his cheeks. The doctor clucked sympathetically and started investigating.

"Well, Doctor?" asked Vinnie after a few minutes had passed. "What's the diagnosis?"

"It's not completely clear, darling," admitted the proctologist, "but the tea leaves recommend a Caribbean cruise for the two of us."

□ □ □

What's really selling on Christopher Street these days?

Designer urns.

□ □ □

Heard about the new gay sitcom?

It's called "Leave It, It's Beaver."

□ □ □

Beset with grief, a poor homosexual had just found out that he had AIDS. "What am I going to do?" pleaded the man, after his doctor had reviewed the prognosis.

"I think you should go to Mexico and live it up. Drink the water and eat all the Mexican cuisine you can get your hands on, including raw fruits and vegetables," advised the doctor.

"Oh, God, Doc, will that cure me?" squealed the gay.

"No," answered the doctor candidly, "but it'll teach you what your asshole is for."

Male

Joe was in the corner bar having a few when his friend Phil dropped in and joined him. It didn't take long for Phil to notice a string hanging out of the back of Joe's shirt collar that his friend kept tugging on.

Finally Phil couldn't contain his curiosity, and asked "What the hell's that string for?"

"Two weeks ago I had a date with that dish, Linda," Joe explained, "and when I got her into the sack, would you believe I couldn't perform? Made me so mad that I tied this string to my dick, and every time I think of how it let me down, I pull the string and make it kiss my ass."

□ □ □

Who's the most popular guy at the nudist camp?

The one who can carry two cups of coffee and a dozen doughnuts at the same time.

□ □ □

Edith and Roberta were hanging out their laundry in their backyards when the talk came around to why Marcia's laundry never got rained on. So when Marcia showed up with her laundry basket, Roberta asked her how come she always seemed to know in advance whether it was going to rain. "Your laundry's never hanging out on those days," she commented in an aggrieved tone.

Marcia leaned over her fence and winked at her two friends. "When I wake up in the morning I look over at Buddy," she explained. "If his penis is hanging over his right leg, I know it's going to be fair weather and I come right out with my laundry. On the other hand, if it's hanging left, for sure it's going to rain, so I hang it up inside."

"Well, smarty-pants," said Edith, "what's the forecast if Buddy's got hard-on?"

"Honey," replied Marcia with a smile, "on a day like *that*, you don't do the *laundry*."

□ □ □

An eight-year-old boy was charged with the rape of a grown woman, and though the charge seemed highly unlikely, the state's evidence was overwhelming. As a last, desperate move, the defense counsel came over to his client on the witness stand, pulled down his pants, and grabbed the little boy's tiny penis. "Ladies and gentlemen," the lawyer cried, gesturing toward the jury box, "surely you cannot believe that such a small, as-yet-undeveloped organ is sexually mature?" Growing more agitated, he went on, "How could it be capable even of erection, let alone the rape of a twenty-eight-year-old—"

"WATCH IT!" yelped the kid from the stand. "One more shake and you'll lose the case."

□ □ □

Hungry for company, a young couple is delighted when a spaceship lands on their very isolated farm and out steps a young, very humanoid Martian couple. They get to talking, and soon the wife invites the Martians to dinner. And over dinner the conversation is so stimulating and all four get along so well that they decide to swap partners for the night.

The farmer's wife and the male Martian get the master bedroom, and when he undresses she sees that his phallus is very small indeed. "What are you going to do with that?" she can't resist asking.

"Watch," he says smartly. He twists his right ear and his penis suddenly grows to eighteen inches in length—but it's still as skinny as a pencil. And again the farmer's wife can't suppress a disparaging comment.

So the Martian twists his left ear, at which his prick grows thick as a sausage. And he and the woman proceed to screw like crazy all night long.

The next morning the Martian couple takes off after cordial farewells, and the farmer turns to his wife. "So how was it?" he asks curiously.

"It was fabulous, really out of this world," reports the wife with a big smile. "How about you?"

"Nothing special," admitted the farmer. "Kinda weird, in fact. All night long she kept playing with my ears."

□ □ □

The customer came up to the pharmacist indignantly. "Last Friday I ordered twelve dozen rubbers," he said angrily, "and when I got home I found I'd been shorted a dozen."

"Gee," said the pharmacist drily, "I hope I didn't ruin your weekend."

□ □ □

When sixteen-year-old Gary came home with the news that he'd gotten laid for the first time, his mother was less than pleased. Slapping him across the face, she sent him off to his room without any supper. When Gary's father got home and heard the news, he went up to see his son.

"Well, Gary," he admonished, secretly pleased, "I hope you learned something from this experience."

"You bet I did," admitted his son. "Next time I won't tell Mom, and I'll use Vaseline. My ass is killing me!"

□ □ □

Hear about the young boy whose mother caught him jerking off in the bathroom?

She told him to stop because he'd go blind . . . and he asked if he could keep going till he needed glasses.

□ □ □

Why do women have such big tits and tight pussys?

Because men have such big mouths and little peckers.

□ □ □

Heard about the "morning-after" pill for men?

It works by changing your blood type.

□ □ □

Jake and Jim were about to head out for another long winter of trapping in the northernmost wilds of Saskatchewan. When they stopped for provisions at the last tiny town, the proprietor of the general store, knowing it was going to be a good many months without female companionship, offered them two boards featuring fur-lined holes.

"We won't be needing anything like that," Jim protested, and Jake shook his head righteously. But the storekeeper pressed the boards on them, pointing out that they could always be burned as firewood.

Seven months later, bearded and gaunt, Jake walked into the general store. After a little chitchat about the weather and the trapping, the storekeeper asked where his partner was.

"I shot the son of a bitch," snarled Jake. "Caught him dating my board."

□ □ □

"Doctor," the man told his physician, "I need a new penis."

The doctor took the request completely in stride. "No problem," he told his patient. "We have a five-incher, a seven-and-a-half-inch model, and a nine-incher. Which do you think would be right for you?"

"The nine-incher," the man decided on the spot. "But would it be possible to take a look at it first?"

"Of course," said the doctor obligingly.

"Gee, Doctor," asked the patient after a few moments, "think I could have it in white?"

□ □ □

One afternoon the red phone on Prime Minister Thatcher's desk rang.

Gorbachev was on the line, asking an urgent favor. "The AIDS virus has reached the USSR, and we are suffering from an acute condom shortage. In fact," the president confessed, "there are none at all to be had in the Moscow pharmacies. Would it be possible for you to ship me 850,000 condoms—immediately—so that we can deal with this public health threat?"

"Why, certainly, Mikhail," replied Mrs. Thatcher gracefully. "Will Friday do?"

"That would be wonderful," sighed the Russian in evident relief. "Oh, and Maggie, one specification: They must be five inches around and nine inches long."

"No problem at all," the Prime Minister assured him breezily. Hanging up, she had her secretary get the largest condom manufacturer in Great Britain on the line, who informed her that a rush order to those specifications would be no problem for his assembly line. "Excellent, excellent," chirped Thatcher. "Now just two more things. . . ."

"Yes, madam?"

"On the condoms must be printed, 'Made in Great Britain,'" Thatcher instructed.

"But of course," the industrialist assured her.

"And 'Medium.'"

□ □ □

For Christmas, Freddy got the chemistry set he'd been begging for, and he promptly disappeared with it into the basement. Eventually, his father came down to see how he was doing, and found Freddy, surrounded by test tubes, pounding away at the wall.

"Son, why're you hammering a nail into the wall?" he asked.

"That's no nail, that's a worm," explained Freddy, and showed his dad the mixture in which he'd soaked the worm.

"Tell you what, pal," suggested Freddy's father, his eyes lighting up. "Lend me that test tube and I'll buy you a Toyota."

Needless to say, Freddy handed it over, and the next day when he got home from school he spotted a brand-new Mercedes Benz in the driveway. "Hey, Dad, what's up?" he called, running into the house.

"The Toyota's in the garage," explained his father, "and the Mercedes is from your mom."

□ □ □

One day, Gary went into the local tattoo parlor with a somewhat odd request. He had this great new girlfriend named Wendy, he explained, and while their sex life was dynamite, he was sure it would be even better if he had her name tattooed on his prick.

The tattoo artist did her best to dissuade him, pointing out that it would be very painful, and that most of the time the tattoo would just read "Wy" anyway. But Gary was undeterred, and went ahead with the tattoo. Sure enough, Wendy was crazy about the tattoo, and their sex grew even wilder and more frequent. Gary was a happy man.

One day he was downtown and had to take a leak in a public bathroom. At the next urinal was a big black guy, and when Gary looked over he was surprised to see "Wy" on this guy's penis as well. "How about that!" he exclaimed. "Say, is your girlfriend's name Wendy, too?"

"Dream on," answered the black guy. "Mine says 'Welcome to Jamaica and Have a Nice Day.'"

□ □ □

The voluptuous blonde was enjoying a stroll around Plato's Retreat, arrogantly examining everyone's equipment before making her choice. In one room she happened against a scrawny, bald fellow with thick glasses, and to complete the picture, his penis was a puny four inches in length.

Checking it out with a sneer, the blonde snickered, "Just who do you think you're going to please with *that*?"

"Me," he answered, looking up with a grin.

□ □ □

A man walked into a bar and started up a conversation with an attractive woman. Pretty soon, he confided that he was recently divorced, "My wife and I just weren't sexually compatible," he explained, "I wanted to experiment . . . you know, try new things, but my wife just wasn't into it. Nice girl, but totally traditional."

The woman's eyes widened as she listened to this tale of marital incompatibility. "That's pretty amazing," she said. "I got divorced a year ago myself, for the same reason. My husband was a total stick-in-the-mud when it came to experimenting sexually." Dropping her voice to a whisper, she confessed to her new acquaintance, "He didn't even like me to be on top."

"Wow, this is *great*!" exclaimed the guy. "You and I are really on the same wavelength. What do you say we go back to my place and get it on?"

"Fine by me," she agreed.

Back at his apartment he issued very specific instructions. "Here's what I want you to do. Take off all your clothes, climb up on my bed, get on your hands and knees, and count to ten."

She obeyed exactly. "Ten," she called out, tingling with excitement. Nothing happened. "Yoo hoo . . . ten," she called sweetly. Then, "I'm waiting. . . ."

"Jeez, I'm sorry," blurted her new acquaintance. "I got off already. I just shat in your purse."

□ □ □

Jack was delighted by the opportunity to use the golf course at the swank country club, and even more so when he hit a hole-in-one on the eighth hole. As he bent over to take his ball out of the cup, a genie popped out. "This club is so exclusive that my magical services are available to anyone who hits a hole-in-one on this hole," the genie explained. "Any wish you desire shall be granted."

"How about that!" Jack was thrilled, and immediately requested a bigger dick.

"Your wish is granted," intoned the genie solemnly, and disappeared down the hole in a puff of incense.

The golfer went on down the green, and as he walked, he could feel his penis slowly lengthening. As the game progressed, Jack could feel it growing and growing, down his thigh, out his shorts leg, down past his knee. "Maybe this wasn't such a great plan after all," muttered Jack to himself, and headed back to the eighth hole with a bucket of balls. Finally he managed a hole-in-one, and by the time he went to collect the ball, he had to hold up the head of his dick to keep it from dragging on the ground.

Out popped the genie. "This club is so exclusive that my magical services are available to anyone who hits a hole-in-one on this hole. Any wish you—"

"Yeah, yeah, yeah," interrupted Jack. "Could you make my legs longer?"

□ □ □

A certain couple loved to compete with each other, comparing achievements in every aspect of their lives: salaries, athletic abilities, social accomplishments, and so on. Everything was a contest, and the husband sank into a deep depression because he had yet to win a single one. Finally, he sought professional counsel, explaining to the shrink that while he wouldn't mind losing once in a while, his unbroken string of defeats had him pretty down.

"Simple enough. All we have to do is devise a game that you can't possibly lose." The shrink thought for a moment, then proposed a pissing contest. "Whoever can pee higher on the wall wins—and how could any woman win?"

Running home, the husband called up, "Darling, I've got a new game!"

"Oooh, I love games," she squealed, running down the stairs. "What is it?"

"C'mon out here," he instructed, pulling her around to the patio. "We're going to stand here, piss on the wall, and whoever makes the highest mark wins."

"What fun! I'll go first." The woman proceeded to lift her dress, then her leg, and pee on the wall about six inches up from the ground. She turned to him expectantly.

"Okay, now it's my turn." The beleaguered husband eagerly unzipped his fly, pulled out his penis, and was just about to pee when his wife interrupted.

"Hang on a sec," she called out. "No hands allowed!"

□ □ □

Mort knew he was probably oversensitive about the problem, but the fact was that his eyes bulged out. He went to doctor after doctor, but none seemed to know of any treatment, and in desperation he looked up "Eyes Bulging Out" in the Yellow Pages. Sure enough, a doctor was listed, and a few days later Mort found himself sitting on a vinyl couch in a seedy waiting room. A little nervous about being the only patient, he reminded himself how rare the condition was and that the doctor *was* a specialist.

At long last, he was admitted to the doctor's office and examined. The doctor leaned back and informed him that there was a remedy, but not an easy one. "I must cut your balls off," he said.

Mort's eyes bulged out even more as he headed for the door. But after a few weeks of thinking it over, Mort acknowledged that his bulging eyes were what kept him from getting laid in the first place, so he decided to go ahead with the operation. So he returned for the operation, and sure enough, his eyeballs sunk back into their sockets most agreeably. In fact, he looked not only normal but actually rather handsome.

Delighted, he thanked the doctor profusely, and decided to treat his remodeled self to a new suit. "Charcoal gray pinstripe," he instructed the tailor. "Medium lapel, no cuffs."

"Fine," said the tailor, nodding. "Come back on Tuesday."

"Aren't you going to measure me?" asked Mort.

"Nah. I've been at this over thirty years; I can tell your size just by looking," the tailor assured him.

"That's impossible," blurted Mort.

"Size forty-two jacket, right?"

"Yes," admitted Mort, amazed.

"Thirty-two-inch inseam, right?"

Mort nodded, dumbstruck.

"Thirty-six-inch waist?"

Again Mort nodded.

"And you wear size forty underwear, right?" concluded the tailor with a smile.

"Nope!" Mort told him. "Thirty-four."

"Listen, you can't fool me," said the tailor wearily. "Don't even *try* to put one over."

"I'm telling you, I wear size thirty-four underwear," Mort insisted.

"You *can't* wear size thirty-four underwear," protested the exasperated tailor. "Your eyes would bulge out of their sockets!"

□ □ □

Joe and Moe went outside to take a leak, and Joe confessed, "I wish I had one like my cousin Junior. He needs four fingers to hold his."

Moe looked over and pointed out, "But you're holding *yours* with four fingers."

"I know," said Joe with a sigh, "but I'm peeing on three of them."

□ □ □

Ohrenstein was less than pleased with the doctor's remedy for the constant fatigue that was plaguing him. "Give up sex completely, Doctor?" he screamed. "I'm a young guy. How can you expect me to just go cold turkey?"

"So get married and taper off gradually."

□ □ □

When Ernie walked into the pharmacy and asked for rubbers, the girl behind the counter asked politely, "What size, please?"

"Gee, I don't know," answered Ernie, a little flustered, so she instructed him to use the fence out back to determine the correct size. And as he walked out the back door, she ran out a side door and behind the fence.

The fence had three holes in it.

Putting his penis in the first hole, Ernie felt capable hands gently stroking it. Reluctantly, he pulled it out, inserted it in the second hole, and within seconds felt a warm, wet pussy at work on the other side of the fence. Groaning with pleasure, he managed to pull out and stick it through the third hole. There he felt an expert set of lips and tongue give him the blow job of his dreams. Jumping up, the salesgirl hurried back behind the counter and was standing there smiling when Ernie staggered back through the door.

"Your size, sir?" she asked politely.

"Forget the rubbers," he grunted. "Just gimme three yards of that fence."

□ □ □

After the birth of his third child, Warner decided to have a vasectomy. During the operation, one of his testicles accidentally fell on the floor, and before the nurse could scoop it back up, the doctor had stepped on it. Unfazed, the doctor simply asked the nurse for a small onion, which he proceeded to suture inside the scrotum.

Two weeks later Warner was back for his post-op checkup. "How's it going?" asked the doctor.

"I gotta tell you, I'm having some problems," admitted the patient.

"Such as?"

"Well, Doc, every time I take a leak, my eyes water;

every time I come, I get heartburn; and every time I pass a Burger King, I get a hard-on!"

□ □ □

Jose cracked up when he came home and found his wife ironing her brassiere. "Why bother?" he asked, wiping tears of laughter off his cheeks. "You got nothing to put in it."

"Is that so?" she shot back. "I iron your shorts, too, don't I?"

□ □ □

Casey made an appointment with a sex therapist and explained that he and his wife were unable to achieve simultaneous climax. "It's not a terrible problem, Doctor," he admitted, "but isn't there something I could do about it?"

The therapist confided that he and his wife had had the same problem, which he'd solved by hiding a pistol under his pillow. "When I was about to come, I reached for the gun and fired a shot, and Doreen climaxed with me. Come back next week and tell me how it works for you."

That very night the therapist got a call from the county hospital and rushed over to the emergency room. "What happened, Casey?" he cried, catching sight of his patient writhing in pain on an examining table, clutching a bloodsoaked towel to his groin.

Wincing, Casey explained that he'd gone right out to purchase a .45, hid it under the pillow, and started making love to his wife. "And when I was about to come, I grabbed the gun and fired."

"So?" pursued the doctor.

"She shat in my face and bit off the end of my dick."

□ □ □

What does a man have in his pants that a woman doesn't want in her face?

Wrinkles!

□ □ □

Female

What do you get when you cross an elephant and a prostitute?

A hooker who does it for peanuts and won't ever forget you.

□ □ □

What does a cow have four of and a woman have two of?

Feet.

□ □ □

A young couple hadn't been married for long when, one morning, the man came up behind his wife as she got out of the shower and grabbed her by the buttocks. "Y'know, honey," he said smugly, "if you firmed these up a little bit, you wouldn't have to keep using your girdle."

Her feelings were so hurt that she refused to speak to him for the rest of the day.

Only a week later, he again stepped into the bathroom just as she was drying off from her shower. Grabbing both breasts, he said, "Y'know, honey, if you firmed these up a bit, you wouldn't have to keep wearing a bra."

The young wife was infuriated, but had to wait till

the next morning to exact her revenge. Waiting till her husband stepped out of the shower, she grabbed him by the penis and hissed, "Y'know, honey, if you firmed this up a little bit, I wouldn't have to keep using your brother."

□ □ □

What does a woman say after her third orgasm?

You mean you don't *know*?

□ □ □

"Say," said Lucille one day over lunch, "weren't you going to go out with that guy who played the French horn?"

"Yeah," said Diane, stirring her ice tea.

"You were really looking forward to it, I remember. How'd it go?" Lucille leaned forward eagerly.

"Actually, he was a pretty nice guy," volunteered Diane reluctantly. "But there was one real problem. . . ."

"Oh, really?"

"Every time he kissed me, he wanted to shove his fist up my ass."

□ □ □

The newlyweds undressed and got into bed. "Sweetheart," asked the new wife, "could you please hand me that jar of Vaseline over there?"

"Baby, you aren't going to need any Vaseline," he growled amorously. But at her insistence he handed it over, and she proceeded to smear it liberally all over her crotch.

After watching this procedure, the husband asked the wife for a favor. "Remember that long string of pearls I gave you for an engagement present? Could you get them out of the bureau drawer for me?"

"Of course, lover," replied his bride, "but whatever do you want them for?"

"Well," he explained, looking down at the Vaseline smeared all over her, "if you think I'm going into a mess like that without chains, you're crazy!"

□ □ □

What's the difference between pussy and cunt?

A pussy is soft, warm, inviting . . . and a cunt is the person who owns it.

□ □ □

What's the ultimate in embarrassment for a woman?

When her Ben-Wa balls set off the metal detector at the airport.

□ □ □

"I do happen to need somebody," admitted the owner of the hardware store to the unimpressive-looking man who was interested in a job. "But tell me, can you sell?"

"Of course," was the confident reply.

"I mean really *sell*," reiterated the shopkeeper.

"You bet," said the young man.

"I'll show you what I mean," said the owner, going over to a customer who had just walked in and asked for grass seed. "We're having a very special sale on lawn mowers," he told the customer. "Could I interest you in one?"

"What do I need a lawn mower for?" protested the customer. "I don't even have any grass yet."

"Maybe not," said the owner agreeably, "but all that seed's going to grow like crazy some day and then you'll need a lawn mower in the worst way. And you won't find them on sale in midsummer, that's for sure."

"I guess you've got a point," admitted the fellow. "Okay, I'll take a lawn mower, too."

"Think you can do that?" asked the storekeeper of his new employee after he'd written up the bill. The man nodded. "Okay, good. Now I have to run to the bank. I'll only be gone for a few minutes, but while I'm gone I want you to sell, sell, sell."

The new guy's first customer was a woman who came over and asked where the tampons were.

"Third aisle over, middle of the second shelf."

When she came to the counter to pay, he leaned over and said, "Hey, you wanna buy a lawn mower? They're on sale."

"Why on earth would I want a lawn mower?" she asked, eyeing him suspiciously.

"Well, you aren't going to be getting laid," he blurted, "so you might as well mow the lawn."

□ □ □

With one look at his voluptuous new patient, all the gynecologist's professional ethics went right out the window. Instructing her to undress completely, he began to stroke the soft skin of her inner thigh. "Do you know what I'm doing?" he asked softly.

"Checking for any dermatological abnormalities, right?"

"Right," crooned the doctor, beginning to fondle her breasts and gently pinch her nipples. "And now?"

"Looking for any lumps that might be cancerous."

"Right you are," reassured the doctor, placing her feet in the stirrups, pulling out his cock, and entering her. "And do you know what I'm doing now?"

"Yup," she said, looking down. "Contracting herpes."

□ □ □

What's black and hairy and fell off the wall?

Humpty Cunt!

□ □ □

Leonard desperately wanted to become a doctor and had really crammed for his medical boards, so he wasn't in the least fazed by the question: "Name the three advantages of breast milk."

Quickly he wrote, "1) It contains the optimum balance of nutrients for the newborn child." He added, "2) As it is contained within the mother's body, it is protected from germs and helps develop the child's immune system." Then Leonard was stumped. Sitting back and racking his brains until he'd broken a sweat, he finally scribbled, "3) It comes in such nice containers."

□ □ □

Two law partners can't resist hiring a gorgeous young receptionist, and despite promises to the contrary, neither can resist going to bed with her. And not too long afterward their worst fears are realized: the blushing receptionist announces that she's pregnant. No one knows who the father is, and the partners are in a total quandary. So toward the end of the pregnancy they decide to chip in and send the girl off to Florida to have the baby.

Several months go by with no news, and finally one of the partners feels so guilty that he hops on a flight to Miami to go check on the young mother. The next night the phone rings in their New York office.

"How is she?" asks his partner.

"Oh, she's fine," was the breezy answer, "but I've got some bad news and some good news."

"Oh yeah? What's the good news?"

"Well, like I said, Jeannette's fine. And she had twins."

"So what's the bad news?" asked the partner from New York.

"Mine died."

□ □ □

What's the definition of eternity?

The length of time between when *you* come and *she* leaves.

□ □ □

Sam and Cindy grew up next door to each other, and as they grew older each constantly tried to one-up the other. If Sam got a jungle gym, Cindy got a swing set, and so on, until the contest became a very expensive one for both sets of parents. Finally Sam's father asked what was going on, and when Sam explained it, a big grin came over his face.

Next Saturday, Cindy whizzed down the sidewalk on a brand new tricycle. "Nyaah, nyaah," she taunted, "look what I've got."

"So?" retorted Sam. "I've got something you'll never have—look!" And he pulled down his pants and showed her.

Realizing she'd been outdone, Cindy ran into her house sobbing. Her father picked her up and tried to comfort her. Getting the whole story out of her, he smiled and whispered something in her ear.

The next day Sam spotted Cindy in the backyard and decided to rub it in. "I've got one of these and you don't," he teased, pulling his pants down again.

"Big deal," said Cindy haughtily, pulling her skirt up and her underpants down. "My Daddy says that with one of *these* I can have as many of *those* as I want."

□ □ □

What would be one of the best things about electing a woman President?

We wouldn't have to pay her as much!

□ □ □

Did you hear about the girl who was so fat she couldn't get out of bed?

She kept rocking herself back to sleep.

□ □ □

The night before her wedding Maria pulled her mother aside for an intimate little chat. "Mom," she confided, "I want you to tell me how I can make my new husband happy."

The bride's mother took a deep breath. "Well, my child," she began, "when two people honor and respect each other, love can be a very beautiful thing."

"I know how to fuck, Mom," interrupted the girl. "I want you to teach me how to make lasagna."

□ □ □

Who enjoys sex more, the man or the woman?

The woman.

How can I prove it?

When your ear itches and you put your little finger in and wiggle it around and take it out again, what feels better, your finger or your ear?

□ □ □

Why do women have two sets of lips?

So they can piss and moan at the same time.

□ □ □

An amateur golfer playing in his first tournament was delighted when a beautiful girl came up to him after the round and suggested he come over to her place for a while. The fellow was a bit embarrassed to explain that he really couldn't stay all night but that he'd be glad to come over for a while. Twenty minutes later they were in her bed making love. And when it was over, he got out of bed and started getting dressed.

"Hey," called the girl from beneath the covers, "where do you think you're going? A guy like Arnold Palmer wouldn't leave so early."

At that the golfer stripped off his clothes and jumped on top of her. Once they'd made love a second time, he got out of bed and put his pants back on.

"What are you up to?" she called. "A real man like Jack Nicklaus wouldn't think of leaving now." So the golfer pulled off his pants and screwed her a third time, and afterward he started getting dressed.

"C'mon, you can't leave yet," protested the girl. "Someone like Lee Trevino wouldn't call it a day."

"Lady, would you tell me one thing?" asked the golfer, looking at her very seriously. "What's par for this hole?"

□ □ □

The salesgirl at the Pink Pussycat boutique didn't bat an eye when the customer purchased an artificial vagina. "What're you going to use it for?" she asked.

"None of your business," answered the customer, thoroughly offended.

"Calm down, buddy," soothed the salesgirl. "The only reason I'm asking is that if it's food, we don't have to charge you sales tax."

□ □ □

The first astronaut to land on Mars was delighted to come across a beautiful Martian woman stirring a huge pot over a campfire. "Hi, there," he said casually. "What're you doing?"

"Making babies," she explained, looking up with a winsome smile.

Horny after the long space voyage, the astronaut decided to give it a shot. "That's not the way we do it on Earth," he informed her.

"Oh, really?" The Martian woman looked up from her pot with interest. "How do your people do it?"

"Well, it's hard to describe," he conceded, "but I'd be glad to show you."

"Fine," agreed the lovely Martian maiden, and the two proceeded to make love in the glow of the fire. When they were finished, she asked, "So where are the babies?"

"Oh, they don't show up for another nine months," explained the astronaut patiently.

"So why'd you stop stirring?"

□ □ □

What do you call a female peacock?

A peacunt.

□ □ □

After a few years of marriage the young woman became increasingly dismayed by her diminishing sex life. She tried everything she could think of, from greeting her husband at the door dressed in Saran Wrap to purchasing exotic paraphernalia from a mail-order sex boutique. But none of it had the desired effect on her husband's libido, and finally she persuaded him to consult a hypnotist.

She was delighted that after only a few visits, her husband's ardor was restored to honeymoon dimensions. There was only one annoying side effect: Every so often during lovemaking he would jump up and run out of the room for a minute or two. At first his wife didn't want to rock the boat, but eventually her curiosity overcame her better judgment. Following him into the bathroom, she saw him staring into the mirror, muttering, "She's not my wife . . . . She's not my wife . . . . She's not my wife . . . ."

□ □ □

As he got into bed, the husband was very much in the mood, but was hardly surprised when his wife pushed his hand off her breast. "Lay off, honey. I have a headache."

"Perfect," he responded, without missing a beat. "I was just in the bathroom powdering my dick with aspirin."

□ □ □

What are a woman's three greatest lies?

1) You're the best.
2) You're the biggest.
3) It doesn't always smell that way.

□ □ □

What chain of food stores do prostitutes patronize?

Stop 'n Blow.

□ □ □

Did you hear about the prostitute who failed her driver's test three times?

She couldn't learn to sit up in a car.

□ □ □

The dentist was called away from the dinner table to take an urgent phone call. It was Mr. Tuckerman, explaining that young Junior had gotten himself into quite a fix. "See, he was kissing his girlfriend Corinne, and when my wife and I came back from the movies we found them stuck together."

"I'll come right over, Mr. Tuckerman," said the dentist calmly, "and don't worry about a thing. I have to unlock teenagers' braces all the time."

"Yes, but from an I.U.D?"

□ □ □

When Jackie went to the dentist for the first time in years, she was prepared for bad news. Nevertheless she was a little put out when, after some time, the dentist gasped, "Jesus, what happened to your teeth? They're all gone, and your gums are in terrible shape!"

"If it's such a big problem," Jackie retorted, "then get your face out of my lap."

□ □ □

What do you get when you cross a hooker with a pit bull?

The last blow job of your life.

□ □ □

What do you call an anorexic with a yeast infection?

A quarter-pounder with cheese.

□ □ □

How do you qualify to be the girlfriend of a Hell's Angel?

You have to be able to suck start a Harley.

□ □ □

Did you hear the one about the lady who got pregnant while she was working at the sperm bank?

She was arrested for embezzlement.

□ □ □

Did you hear about the girl who had tits on her back?

She was ugly to look at, but a whole lot of fun to dance with.

□ □ □

Mike was touching up the paint in the bathroom one weekend when the brush slipped out of his hand, leaving a stripe across the toilet seat. So Mike painted the whole seat over and went off to a ball game.

His wife happened to get home early, went upstairs to pee, and found herself firmly stuck to the toilet seat. At six o'clock Mike found her there, furious and embarrassed, but was unable to dislodge her for fear of tearing the skin.

With considerable difficulty Mike managed to get her into the back seat of the car and then into a wheelchair at the county hospital, where she was wheeled into a room and maneuvered, on her knees, onto an examining table. At this point the resident entered and surveyed the scene. "What do you think, Doc?" broke in the nervous husband.

"Nice, very nice," he commented, stroking his chin. "But why the cheap frame?"

Animal

A horny mouse met a giraffe and fell in love with her, and after much entreating on the mouse's part, the giraffe agreed to spend the night with him. So the mouse's best friend was surprised to run across him the next morning looking like hell. "What happened to you?" he asked.

"Between the kissing and the screwing," answered the weary rodent, "I must have run a hundred miles."

□ □ □

What does a black parrot say?

"Polly wanna white woman."

□ □ □

Warren worked for a small mining operation so he was used to the desolate little towns of the Southwest. But when he was sent to Dry Gulch for a couple of months, something seemed strange from the very beginning, and one night in the local saloon he realized what it was. "Say," he said to the bartender, "aren't there any women in this town?"

"Nope," admitted the bartender. "The men here had so little to offer that all the women packed up and left years ago."

Warren's face fell. "That's pretty grim. What do the guys do on a Saturday night?"

"They do it with pigs," was the bartender's cool reply.

"Yecch!" Warren retched and left in disgust. But after a few weeks of total boredom he found himself back in the saloon, and casually inquired as to where the pigs in question were to be found.

The bartender was free with the information. "Just behind the farmhouse at the top of the hill."

One look at the pigs slopping around in the muddy pen was almost enough to send Warren back down the hill. But just as he was turning away, he spotted the cutest pig you could ever hope to see, with big brown eyes, a bow on the top of her head, and not a bit of mud on her little pink trotters. Quite smitten, he led her out of the sty, down the hill, and into the saloon for a drink. But to Warren's surprise his arrival caused quite a commotion, and all the seedy types backed away from him into the far corners of the bar. "Hey, what's up?" asked Warren angrily of the bartender. "You told me everyone in the place goes out with pigs."

"True enough," admitted the bartender, "but we weren't expecting you to take the *sheriff's* girl."

□ □ □

One afternoon a farmer was telling his neighbor how to screw a sheep. "The trick," he shared with his friend, "is to sneak up behind her, grab ahold of her rear legs, spread 'em and lift 'em up to your dick."

"That sounds easy enough," the other farmer said, "but how do you kiss her?"

□ □ □

Why did the farmer name the unwanted puppies Un, Deux, Trois, and Quatre?

Because when he threw them in the lake, Un, Deux, Trois and Quatre sank.

□ □ □

Why do elephants drink?

It helps them forget.

□ □ □

A man with a frog perched on top of his head goes to see a doctor.

"What seems to be the problem?" the physician asks.

"My ass," the frog responds, to the amazement of the doctor.

"And . . . uh . . . what's wrong with your ass?" the doctor inquires further, somewhat nonplussed.

"Would you believe," complains the frog, "this started as a wart?"

□ □ □

What's green and leaps into bed?

A prostitoad.

□ □ □

The bartender was dumbfounded when a gorilla came in and asked for a martini, but he couldn't think of any reason not to serve the beast. And he was even more amazed to find the gorilla coolly holding out a ten-dollar bill when he returned with the libation.

As he walked over to the cash register, he decided to try something. He rang up the sale, headed back to the animal, and handed it a dollar in change. Nonplussed, the gorilla just sat there sipping his martini.

Finally the bartender couldn't take it any more. "You know," he offered, "we don't get too many gorillas in here."

"At nine bucks a drink," the gorilla returned, "I'm not surprised."

□ □ □

At their annual football game, the big animals are really trouncing the little animals with a tremendous offensive game. At halftime the score is 33–0, and it's only with considerable effort that the little animals manage to stop the opposition's kickoff return on the twenty-two-yard line. On the first down, the big animals send the hippopotamus around the right end, but as soon as he gets to the line of scrimmage—BANG!—he's stopped cold.

Back in the huddle, the squirrel, captain of the little critters, says, "Say, that was great! Who stopped the hippo, anyway?"

"Me," said the centipede.

On the second down, the rhino charges around the left end, but he too is stopped cold at the line of scrimmage. "Terrific," cheers the squirrel. "Who did it this time?"

"Me," said the centipede.

On the third down the big animals send the elephant right up the middle, but he doesn't get one yard before he's knocked flat on his back. "Was that you again?" asked the squirrel of the bug.

"Yup," said the centipede modestly.

"Well, where the hell were you during the first half?" demanded the captain.

"Taping my ankles."

□ □ □

What do you get when you cross an elephant with a prostitute?

A two-ton pickup.

□ □ □

What's scarier than a pit bull with AIDS?

The guy who gave it to him.

□ □ □

A snake had the misfortune to be born blind, and though he managed to forage successfully, he was very lonely. So he was delighted to make the acquaintance of a little mole—which was very nearly blind, as such creatures are—who offered to be his friend.

They got together nearly every day, and finally the snake mustered up his courage to ask the mole a question. "We have become dear friends, and yet I have no idea what you look like," he pointed out. "Would you mind if I coiled myself around you very gently so I could get an image of you?"

"Not at all," replied the mole graciously, and soon found himself in the center of a mountain of snake.

"Why, you are soft and furry, with a pointy little nose surrounded by bristly whiskers. Could it be that you are a mole?" asked the snake.

"I am indeed," answered the mole. "And you—you are cold and slimy and are covered with scales and have no balls."

"Ssssshit," hissed the snake, "I must be a lawyer."

□ □ □

Why are dogs better than kids?

When you get sick of your dog, you can put it to sleep.

□ □ □

What did one Hawaiian shark say to the other?

"Oh, no—not airplane food again."

□ □ □

Myron's mother was very hard to please, but one year he thought hard and finally came up with a truly inspired birthday present: a gorgeous parrot that spoke six languages. He paid the exorbitant price and ordered the bird delivered to her apartment in an ornate antique cage on the appointed day.

That evening he came by for the birthday dinner. "So, Mom, did you get my present?" he asked casually.

"Yes, Myron, I did. And I must say it's cooked up very nicely."

"You didn't cook it!" gasped Myron. "Mom, that bird cost me fifteen hundred dollars. And it spoke English, Portuguese, Mandarin, Urdu, Arabic, and Russian!"

"Now, Myron," the old woman chided, shaking her head, "if it really spoke all those languages, why didn't it say something?"

□ □ □

Shirley had always wanted to see Australia, so she saved up her money and went off on a two-week tour. And she'd only been there three days when she fell head over heels in love with a kangaroo. So she blithely disregarded the advice of her tour guide and companions, had an aboriginal priest perform a wedding ceremony, and brought the new husband back to her house in the Midwest.

But she found that the course of new love was not without its problems, and in a few months decided to consult a marriage counselor. "Frankly, in your case it's not hard to put my finger on the heart of the problem," pronounced the counselor almost immediately. "Besides the obvious ethnic and cultural differences between you and your husband, it's clearly going to be impossible to establish genuine lines of communication with a kangaroo."

"Oh, that's not it at all," Shirley broke in. "My husband and I communicate perfectly—except in bed. There it's nothing but hop on, hop off, hop on, hop off. . ."

□ □ □

"I hope you can help me, Dr. Berg," said the woman to a podiatrist. "My feet hurt me all the time."

The doctor asked her to walk down the hall and back while he observed, and when she sat back down he pointed out that she was extremely bowlegged. "Do you know if this is a congenital problem?"

"Oh, no, it developed quite recently. You see, I've been screwing doggie fashion a lot."

"Well I'd recommend trying another sexual position," said the doctor, slightly taken aback.

"No way," she replied tartly. "That's the only way my Doberman will fuck."

□ □ □

"Now cheer up, Paul," soothed his buddy Bill over a couple of Budweisers. "You and Louise seem to be doing just fine. And it's a little silly for you to be jealous of a German shepherd, frankly. After all, you work all day and you live out in the sticks. That dog's good company for Louise."

"Good company!" snorted Paul, nearly spilling his beer. "Hey, the other night I caught her douching with Gravy Train."

□ □ □

Did you hear about the lion who consulted an eminent Beverly Hills psychiatrist?

The king of the beasts complained that every time he roared, he had to sit though a two-hour movie.

Religious

Old Timothy O'Day was clearly on his deathbed. So his son, Liam, was completely taken aback when the old man plucked at his sleeve, drew him close, and said, "My boy, it's time for you to go for the minister."

"But Dad," gasped Liam, "what on earth would a good Catholic like yourself be wanting with the Protestants at a time like this—meaning no disrespect, of course."

"Get the minister," ordered O'Day fiercely, and after a few more sputtering protests, his son hurried off to honor what might be his father's last request. He was back with the Reverend Wilson within forty-five minutes, and listened in dismay outside the door as the minister converted his father and administered the Protestant last rites.

His distress, however, paled beside that of Father McGuire, who hurried up the stairs past the departing Reverend Wilson. "Tim, Tim, *why*?" he cried, bursting into the old man's room. "We went to St. Joseph's together. We were altar boys at Our Lady of the Sacred Heart. I was there at your First Communion and you saw the first Mass I performed. How in the world could you do such a thing?"

"Paddy," said old O'Day, leaning back against his

pillows, "I figured if somebody had to go, better one of them than one of us."

□ □ □

Did you hear about the new Cabbage Patch dolls for atheists' kids?

They're stuffed with catnip and dressed as early Christians.

□ □ □

When the Mother Superior answered the knock at the convent door, she found two leprechauns shuffling their feet on the doorsill. "Aye an' begorrah, Mother Superior," said the foremost one after an awkward pause, "would ye be havin' any leprechaun nuns in your church?"

The nun shook her head solemnly.

The little man shuffled his feet a bit more, then piped up, "An' would there be any leprechaun nuns in the convent?"

"No, my boys," said the Mother Superior gravely.

"Ye see, laddy," cried the leprechaun, whirling around to his companion triumphantly. "I *told* you ye been fucking a penguin!"

□ □ □

Things were a little slow in heaven one evening, so Moses suggested to Jesus that they go down to earth and visit a whorehouse.

"You go first, Jesus," Moses said, as he settled down in the waiting room with a magazine.

To Moses' amazement, Jesus walked out of the bedroom thirty seconds later. "Boy, that was fast," the prophet commented.

"I'm such a jerk," Jesus replied in disgust. "The woman opened her legs and showed me her hole, but before I could stop myself, I healed the damned thing closed."

□ □ □

The priest became friends with the rabbi whose synagogue was across the street from his church, and one day he couldn't help remarking on the fact that the church was in perfect repair, while the synagogue needed a new roof and was generally dilapidated. "I don't seem to be able to get a penny out of my congregation," confessed the rabbi, "wealthy though they are. And while your parishioners are mostly blue-collar workers, you're obviously rolling in money."

"I'll show you how I do it," offered the priest generously, and beckoned for the rabbi to follow him into the confession booth.

Soon a penitent entered. "Father, I have sinned," she murmured. "I have committed adultery."

"Three Hail Marys and ten dollars in the collection box," ordered the priest. And so it went; for each of his sinning parishioners, the priest prescribed some Hail Marys and a donation. Eventually the priest turned to the rabbi and suggested that he handle the next one. "Professional courtesy," he said with a smile. "I'm sure you've gotten the point."

So the rabbi was behind the screen when the next person came into the booth. "Father, I committed adultery three times last week," she confessed in a whisper.

"Thirty dollars and nine Hail Marys," ordered the rabbi.

"But, Father, I only have twenty-five dollars," she admitted in great distress.

"That's all right," the rabbi consoled her, not missing a beat. "Put the twenty-five in the collection box and go home and do it again. We've got a special this week—four for the price of two and a half."

□ □ □

An angry crowd was milling around Jesus as he began his ascent up the hill to Calvary, and he got nervous when he saw them picking up rocks from the pathway. Raising his hands, Jesus intoned, "Let he who is without sin cast the first stone."

A hush fell over the crowd. Then—thunk!—a rock hit him on the temple. "Ma," said Jesus, flinching, "you always were a bitch."

□ □ □

When the golfer went to retrieve his ball from deep in the woods, he was startled to come across a witch stirring a huge caldron. Observing the steaming green brew with fascination, he finally asked, "What's in there?"

"A magic brew," hissed the witch. "One swig and you'll play better golf than anyone in the world. You'll be unbeatable."

"Fantastic!" exclaimed the golfer, his eyes lighting up. "Let me have some."

"Hold your horses," cackled the hag gleefully. "There's a catch. You'll pay for it with your sex life: It'll become the worst in the world."

The man stopped to think it over. "No sex . . . great golf . . ." he mused. "Give me a cup."

Finding his ball, the golfer headed out of the woods, finished his game in no time, and went on to whip the club champion that afternoon. Soon he became the best golfer in the country, constantly on tour, but a year later he found himself on the same course. Out of curiosity he went back into the woods, and sure enough the witch was still there, stirring her brew. "You again," she wheezed, looking up blearily. "How's your golf game?"

He recited his latest triumphs on the circuit.

"And your sex life?" The witch tittered malevolently, but her expression changed to surprise when he answered, "Not bad."

"Not bad? How many times have you gotten laid this year?" The witch's curiosity had clearly gotten the best of her.

"Three, maybe four times," answered the golfer.

"And you call that 'not bad'?" retorted the witch.

"Actually, no," said the golfer modestly, "not for a Catholic priest with a very small congregation."

□ □ □

Old Mrs. Watkins awoke one spring morning to find that the river had flooded not only her basement but the whole first floor of her house. And, looking out her bedroom window, she saw that the water was still rising.

Two men in a passing rowboat shouted up an invitation to row to safety with them.

"No, thank you," answered Mrs. Watkins tartly. "The Lord will provide." The men shrugged and rowed on.

By evening the water had risen so much that Mrs. Watkins was forced to climb out onto her roof, where she was spotted by a cheerful man in a motorboat. "Don't worry, lady," he yelled across the water, "I'll pick you right up."

"Please don't bother—the Lord will provide." And Mrs. Watkins turned her back on her would-be rescuer. "Suit yourself," he said, buzzing off.

Pretty soon Mrs. Watkins was forced to take refuge on her chimney, the only part of her house which was still above water. Fortunately a Red Cross cutter came by on patrol. "Jump in, lady; we'll save you," urged a rescue worker.

"No, thank you," said Mrs. Watkins. "The Lord will provide." So the boat went on, the water rose, and Mrs. Watkins drowned. Dripping wet and quite annoyed, she came through the pearly gates and demanded to see God. "What happened?" she demanded furiously. "I thought the Lord would *provide*."

"For cryin' out loud, lady," answered God wearily, "I sent *three boats.*"

□ □ □

The Pope decided to visit America and was gratified to see a huge crowd waiting for him at JFK Airport. But it was disconcerting to hear them chanting, "Elvis! Elvis! Elvis!" as he stepped down from the plane. "Oh, my children, thank you," he said, bowing his head modestly. "But I am not Elvis."

No one seemed to hear him, and he was ushered into a white stretch limo with "Elvis" written in diamonds on the doors. "Bless you," he said to the sequined chauffeur, "but I am not Elvis."

When the limo pulled up to the Waldorf, it had to make its way through a huge crowd crammed behind police barricades, all chanting, "Elvis! Elvis! Elvis!"

Shaking his head, the Pope followed his luggage to the most sumptuous suite in the hotel. As he was unpacking, the door behind him opened and in walked three lovely women clad in the scantiest of negligees. The Pope looked them over for a moment or two, cleared his throat, and began to sing, "Well, it's one for the money, two for the show . . . ."

□ □ □

Father Harris was motoring along a country lane in his parish on a spring afternoon when all of a sudden he got a flat tire. Exasperated, the priest stopped his car, got out and assessed the damage. Luckily, a four-wheel drive jeep rounded the bend and pulled to a stop behind the crippled vehicle. The door to the jeep opened and out stepped a powerful hulk of a man. "Good afternoon, Father," greeted the stranger. "Can I give you a hand?"

"Heaven be praised," rejoiced the priest. "As you can see, my son, I have a flat tire, and I must admit I've never changed one before."

"Don't worry about it, Father. I'll take care of it." And without skipping a beat, the bruiser picked up the front of the car with one hand and removed the lug nuts from the base of the flat tire with the other. "Why don't you get the spare from the trunk?" he asked.

"Why, ahh, yes, of course, my son," stuttered the amazed Father Harris. The priest rolled the spare around to the strongman, who casually lifted it up with his free hand, maneuvered it into place, and proceeded to tighten the lug nuts.

"Do you need the wrench?" the Father queried.

"That's okay," the fellow told him. "These nuts are as tight as a nun's cunt."

"Hmmm," mused Father Harris. "I'd better get the wrench."

□ □ □

What do you have when you sign up a hooker and two nuns for your football team?

One wide receiver and two tight ends.

□ □ □

What does the inscription INRI on the Cross stand for?

I'm Nailed Right In.

□ □ □

The priest leaned closer to hear the girl's confession. "So me and my cousin were alone in the house," she continued, "and we went up to my bedroom . . ."

"Go on, my child," coaxed the priest gently.

"I lay down on the bed and Joe got on top of me and put his hand on my . . . on my . . ."

"Go on."

"On my pussy," stammered the girl, blushing behind the screen. "And touched me and touched me until I couldn't help myself."

"Yes, go on," directed the priest.

"I pulled down his pants and his cock popped out, stiff and tall," the girl went on, with a little whimper of shame, "and he began to shove it in me so hard . . ."

"Yes, yes, yes, go on," he urged.

"And then we heard the front door slam—"

"Oh, SHIT!"

□ □ □

What's the worst thing about being an atheist?

You have no one to talk to when you're getting a great blow job.

□ □ □

Seated next to an aged rabbi on a transcontinental flight, the eager young priest couldn't resist the opportunity to proselytize. "You really should think about coming over to the Roman Catholic faith, being welcomed into the arms of the Holy Father," he enthused. "It is the only true faith, you know—only those who believe in the Sacraments shall be admitted to the Kingdom of Heaven when they die."

The rabbi nodded indulgently but expressed no interest in the mechanics of conversion, and eventually the young priest fell silent, depressed by his failure. Soon after, the plane ran into a tremendous hurricane, lost power, and crashed into the Illinois countryside. Miraculously the priest was thrown, unhurt, from his seat. When he came to and looked back at the flaming wreckage, the first thing he saw was the rabbi, making the sign of the cross.

Crossing himself and whispering a brief prayer of gratitude, the priest ran over and took his arm. "Praise the Lord!" he babbled joyfully, "You *did* hear the Word after all, didn't you? And just in time for it to comfort you through mortal peril. And you do wish to be saved, to become one of us now. Alleluia!"

"Vat on earth are you talking about?" asked the elderly fellow, still rather dazed.

"Sir, I saw it with my own eyes. As you stepped out of the flames, you made the sign of the cross!"

"Cross? Vat cross?" asked the rabbi irritably. "I was simply checking: spectacles, testicles, vallet and vatch."

□ □ □

Ogilvie worked so hard putting himself through school and starting his own company that he had no time to devote to any sort of social or family life. But when he reached his forties and had succeeded in amassing a considerable fortune, he decided it was time to marry—and that only a virgin would be suitable. He realized the odds were against him, so he decided to adopt a baby girl and have her raised in a monastery in rural England until she was of marriageable age.

Fortunately Ogilvie was a patient man, but even so, sixteen years was a long time to wait. Soon after a dour nun had escorted the lovely young woman across the Atlantic, the marriage had been performed, and Ogilvie had carried her across the threshold of his magnificent house, he was trembling in anticipation. Gently he laid his delicate bride down on the bed, then reached into a drawer and pulled out a tube of K-Y jelly he'd had the forethought to purchase in advance.

"An' what would that be for?" asked the girl curiously.

"So it won't hurt when I enter you, dearest," he explained tenderly.

She dismissed the tube with a wave. "An' why not just spit on your cock the way the monks did?"

Celebrity

Why did Arnold Schwarzenegger and Maria Shriver marry?

So they could breed the first bulletproof Kennedy.

□ □ □

What do you get when you cross a Cabbage Patch doll with the Pillsbury Doughboy?

A bitch with a yeast infection.

□ □ □

Why did Dolly Parton's teeth fall out?

Her dentist couldn't reach them.

□ □ □

Did you hear about the Colonel Khaddafi doll?

Wind it up and it takes Barbie and Ken hostage.

□ □ □

Did you know Gary Hart placed a long-distance call during that weekend in Bimini?

He said, "I've got her in the water, Ted—now what do I do?"

□ □ □

What did the seven dwarfs say when the prince awoke Snow White?

"Guess it's back to jerking off."

□ □ □

Entering his prison cell for the first time, child-abuser Joel Steinberg was introduced to his cellmate, a 6′4″ black serving twenty-five years for rape and manslaughter. "We gonna be in here for a long, long time," commented the cellmate.

With a nervous nod, Steinberg acknowledged that this was so.

"Such a long time that it's kinda like a marriage, wouldn't ya say?"

"Sure," conceded Steinberg.

"And in every marriage there's a husband and a wife, right?" the giant black continued relentlessly.

"Right," Steinberg admitted, breaking into a cold sweat.

"So what you wanna be, de husband or de wife?"

"The husband," blurted Steinberg with a sigh of relief.

"Fine," commented his roommate, settling his huge frame on the bottom bunk bed. "Now get ovah heah and suck yo' wife's dick."

□ □ □

Did you hear Jimmy Swaggart's starting up a new magazine?

It's called *Repenthouse*.

□ □ □

How do Ted Bundy's friends commemorate the anniversary of his death?

They lay a wreath on the fuse box.

□ □ □

What's Billy Martin doing now?
Managing the Angels.

□ □ □

Hear how they buried Martin's casket?
All the umpires kicked dirt over it.

□ □ □

What did Quayle say when he heard about the Berlin Wall?
"Now when are those Chinese going to take down *their* wall?"

□ □ □

What's the worst thing about massacring a thousand Chinese students?
An hour later, you feel like massacring a thousand more.

□ □ □

When Buckwheat grew up and changed his name, what did he decide to call himself?
Kareem of Wheat!

□ □ □

Did you hear that Mel Brooks is putting together a new movie, starring Michael Jackson and Richard Pryor?
It's going to be called *Blazing Sambos!*

□ □ □

What's the difference between Elvis and Salman Rushdie?
Elvis lives.

□ □ □

Heard about Zsa Zsa's new perfume?

It's called "Conviction"—you just slap it on.

□ □ □

The attractive woman turned to the man in the business suit behind her in the elevator. "Excuse me," she asked, "but are you Donald Trump?"

The man cleared his throat. "Yes, as a matter of fact, I am."

"Oh," she gushed, "I've *always* wanted to meet you, Mr. Trump. And now that we're together," she continued throatily, "I'll tell you what I'd like to do: I'm inviting you back to my room, where I'll kneel in front of you and pull out your cock and suck it till you have a giant hard-on and suck it some more until you come all over my face. . . ."

"I don't know," interrupted Trump, thinking it over. "What's in it for me?"

Old Age

How do you know when you're getting old?

When your wife gives up sex for Lent and you don't find out till Easter.

□ □ □

A young woman was walking toward the bus stop when she came across a little old man sitting on the curb, sobbing his heart out. Moved by his grief, the woman bent over and asked him what was so terribly wrong.

"Well, you see," choked the old man, "I used to be married to this awful bitch. She was fat and ugly, never put out, the house was a pigsty, and she spent my money like water. She wasn't even a decent cook. My life was hell."

The young woman clucked sympathetically.

"After thirty years of living hell, she died," the old man went on with a sob, "and I met this beautiful woman. Twenty-eight years old, a body like Sophia Loren and face like an angel, a fabulous cook and housekeeper, the hottest thing in bed you could possibly imagine, and—can you believe it at my age?—crazy over me! She couldn't wait to marry me, and treats me like a prince in my own home."

"This doesn't sound so bad," volunteered the young woman, frankly puzzled.

"I tell you, I'm the luckiest man in the world." The old coot bent over in a racking spasm, convulsed with sorrow.

"Well, then," asked the woman tentatively, "what's to be so unhappy about? Why are you sobbing on the street corner?"

"Because," he sobbed, "I can't remember where I live!"

□ □ □

A tired-looking old prostitute walked into a bar with a pigeon on her head and shouted, "Whoever can guess the weight of this bird can fuck me!"

Way in the back of the bar, a drunk yells, "One thousand pounds!"

"Close enough," she answered cheerfully.

□ □ □

"The doctor said I have the legs of a seventeen-year-old!" announced the old woman triumphantly to her husband.

"Big deal," her husband chuckled sarcastically, "what did he say about your sixty-five-year-old ass?"

"Oh," she replied, "he didn't mention you."

□ □ □

"Excuse me, doctor," asked the nurse, "but why is that old man sticking out his tongue and holding up his middle finger?"

"Simple, nurse," answered the doctor, "I asked him to show me his sexual organs."

□ □ □

"Doctor, I'm losing my sex urge," complained Ruth at her annual checkup.

"Mrs. Beeston, that's understandable at eighty-four," said the doctor, "but tell me: When did you first start noticing this?"

"Last night," she answered, "and then again this morning."

"Aha," said the doctor. "Your problem isn't a diminished sex drive, it's that you're not getting enough. You should be having sex at least fifteen times a month."

Thanking him and heading home, the old woman couldn't wait to report the doctor's prescription to her husband. "Guess what, Pop? He says I need it fifteen times a month!"

Pop put in his teeth and said, "That's just great, honey. Put me down for five."

□ □ □

Herschel was astounded—and a little worried—when Reuben announced his upcoming marriage to a twenty-year-old girl. "At your advanced age," cautioned his friend, "couldn't that be fatal?"

Reuben shrugged philosophically, "If she dies, she dies."

□ □ □

When old Mr. O'Leary died, an elaborate wake was planned. In preparation, Mrs. O'Leary called the undertaker aside for a private little talk. "Please be sure to secure his toupee to his head very securely. No one but me knew he was bald," she confided, "and he'd never rest in peace if anyone found out at this point. But our friends from the old country are sure to hold his hands and touch his head before they're through paying their last respects."

"Rest assured, Mrs. O'Leary," comforted the undertaker. "I'll fix it so that toupee will never come off."

Sure enough, the day of the wake the old timers

were giving O'Leary's ancient corpse quite a going-over, but the toupee stayed firmly in place. At the end of the day, a delighted Mrs. O'Leary offered the undertaker an extra thousand dollars for handling the matter so professionally.

"Oh, I couldn't possibly accept your money," protested the undertaker. "What's a few nails?"

□ □ □

Talking to his friends on the front porch, ninety-two-year-old Ed reports, "I've got my health, my heart is strong, my liver is good, and my mind, knock wood. . . . Who's there?"

□ □ □

Sam wasn't happy about putting his dad in the state nursing home but it was all he could afford—until a lucky investment paid off. The first thing he did with his new-found wealth was to move his father to the best nursing home available.

The old man was astounded by the luxury of his new surroundings. On the first day, he started to list to his right side in front of the television. Instantly a nurse ran over and tactfully straightened him out. Over lunch he started to lean a bit to the left, but within a few seconds a nurse gently pushed him upright again.

That night his son called. "How're you doing, Pop?" he asked eagerly.

"Oh, Sam, it's a wonderful place," said the father. "I've got my own color TV, the food is cooked by a French chef, the gardens look like Versailles, you wouldn't believe."

"Dad, it sounds perfect."

"There's one problem with the place, though, Sammy," the father whispered. "They won't let you fart."

□ □ □

What's the difference between an old man and a penis?

When you hold a penis, the wrinkles disappear.

□ □ □

Just as the elderly woman was turning her Mercedes into a parking space at the mall, she was edged out by a red Firebird. "You've got to be young and fast," jeered the teenaged driver as he jumped out from behind the wheel.

The woman reversed, revved her engine, and rammed the Firebird. As the Mercedes reversed and headed for his car again, the teenager turned and gaped, then ran over and banged on the woman's window. "What the hell do you think you're doing?" he screeched.

She smiled sweetly and explained, "You've got to be old and rich."

□ □ □

Seventy-three-year-old Sol had worked in the garment center all his life, never finding the time to get married. But one day a beautiful seventeen-year-old girl walked into the store and it was love at first sight. Within a month Sol and Rachel were married and on the way to Florida for their honeymoon.

"So how was it?" asked Herschel, Sol's partner, on the couple's return. "Oh, just beautiful," replied a starry-eyed Sol. "The sun, the surf . . . and we made love almost every night, we—"

"Just a minute," interrupted Herschel. "At your age, forgive me for asking, you made love almost every night?"

"Oh, yes," said Sol, "we almost made love Saturday, we almost made love Sunday. . . ."

□ □ □

The retired couple was sitting at the table after their Sunday lunch when the wife looked over and said, "Know what I feel like? An ice cream. Will you go get me one?"

"Okay, honey," said the long-suffering husband, getting up.

"But not just any ice cream," she interrupted. "A sundae."

"Okay, dear, a sundae it is."

"But not just any sundae, a banana split. Should I write it down and put the note in your coat pocket?"

"No, dear," said the husband, pulling on his coat. "You want a special sundae, a banana split."

"Right, but not just any banana split. I want a scoop of chocolate on one side and a scoop of vanilla on the other. Sure you don't want me to write it down?"

"I got it, I got it," said the beleaguered husband, heading for the door.

"But that's not all," she shouted after him. "I want it to be special. I want whipped cream and a cherry on top. Let me write it down for you."

"No, no, no," protested her husband. "You want a special ice cream sundae: a banana split with a scoop of vanilla here, a scoop of chocolate there, some whipped cream, and a cherry on top."

"And don't forget the chopped nuts."

"Chopped nuts," repeated the husband as the door closed after him.

Two hours later the husband returned and put a greasy paper bag on the kitchen table. The wife walked over, looked inside, and saw four bagels. Looking up at him in intense irritation, she snapped, "I knew it—you forgot the cream cheese."

□ □ □

Hear about the old queen who was brought up on charges of having molested a choirboy?

The judge dismissed the case on the grounds that the evidence wouldn't stand up in court.

□ □ □

The well-meaning social worker was seeing if Mrs. Englehardt qualified for admission to the local nursing home, and part of the standard procedure was a test for senility. "And what's this?" she asked sweetly of the old German woman, who was sitting at the dinner table.

"Dot? Dot's a spoon," answered Mrs. Englehardt.

"Very good," said the social worker. "And this?"

"Dot's a fork," answered the old woman.

"*Very* good. And this?" asked the social worker, holding up a knife.

"Dot's a phallic symbol."

□ □ □

Harold saved for years and years for his dream vacation—a weekend in Nevada, where prostitution was legal. However, since Harold worked for barely the minimum wage, the years stretched into decades, and so he was ninety-one when he got off the bus in Reno in front of a glitzy bordello.

Harold tottered up to the front desk. "Isn't this Adelaide's famous Pleasure Palace?" he asked.

"Why, yes," replied the disbelieving receptionist. "How can I help you?"

"Don't you have the most beautiful gals in town lined up and waiting?" Harold quavered. The receptionist nodded. "Well, I'm here to get laid."

"How old are you, Pops?" she asked bluntly.

"I'm ninety-one."

"Ninety-one! Pops, you've *had* it."

"Oh, really?" A disconcerted look passed over the old man's face as his trembling fingers reached for his wallet. "What do I owe you?"

□ □ □

Mrs. Garwood lived up in the hills and had always been healthy as a horse, but as old age approached, she found herself suffering from some "female troubles." Finally she confessed this to her daughter-in-law, who made an appointment with a gynecologist in the city and drove her in.

A wide-eyed Mrs. Garwood lay silent and still as a stone while the doctor examined her. When it was over, she sat up and fixed a beady eye on the physician. "You seem like such a nice young man," she quavered. "But, tell me, does your mother know what you do for a living?"

Miscellaneous

You probably already know what NASA stands for (Need Another Seven Astronauts) but did you know their official drink was changed?

They've switched from Tang to Ocean Spray.

□ □ □

So how many astronauts can you fit in a Honda Civic?

Two in the front seat, three in the back, and seven in the ashtray.

□ □ □

And what's worse than finding glass in your baby food?

Finding astronaut in your tuna fish.

□ □ □

What the difference between an asshole and a rectum?

You can't put your arm around a rectum. [Use accompanying gesture.]

□ □ □

Mrs. Fisher, the sixth-grade teacher, tells the class that today they're going to have a spelling bee. Instructing the first kid to stand up, she asks, "Robert, what does your father do for a living? Say it nice and clearly, and then spell it out."

"My father's a baker," answers Robert. "B-A-K-E-R-R."

"That's not quite right, Robert. Try again," chides Mrs. Fisher gently.

"B-A—" says Robert, thinking hard, "K-E-R."

"Very good. Now, Cecily?"

"Doctor. D-O-C-T-O-R." Cecily sits down smugly.

"Very good. Herbie?"

Herbie stands up and says, "Shiplayer. S-H-I-T—"

"No, Herbie," interrupts Mrs. Fisher. "Try again."

"Ship . . . layer. S-H-I-T—"

"No, no, no. Go to the blackboard and write it out and you'll see your mistake."

As Herbie heads toward the front of the class, Mrs. Fisher turns to the next child, Lenny, who jumps up and says, "My father's a bookie. That's B-double-O-K-I-E and I'll lay you six to one that dope puts 'shit' on the board."

□ □ □

What's LXIX?

Sixty-nine the hard way.

□ □ □

How many actors does it take to change a light bulb?

One hundred. One to change the bulb, and ninety-nine to say, "I could have done that."

□ □ □

A rather scruffy-looking type came into a bank. Reaching the head of the line, he said to the teller, "I wanna open a fucking checking account."

"Certainly, sir," answered the teller, "but there's no need to use that kind of language."

"Couldja move it along lady? I just wanna open a fucking checking account," growled the would-be customer.

"I'll be glad to be of service, sir," said the teller, flushing slightly, "but I would appreciate not being spoken to in that way."

"Just lemme open a fucking checking account, okay?"

"I'm afraid I'm going to have to speak to the branch manager," said the flustered teller, slipping off her stool and returning shortly with a dapper middle-aged man who asked how he could be of service.

"I just won the ten-million-dollar lottery," snarled the man, "and all I wanna do is open a fucking checking account."

"I see," said the manager sympathetically. "And this bitch is giving you trouble?"

□ □ □

The avid golfer was out on the course with his wife one day. He played a shot on the fifth that sliced so badly that it ended up in the gardener's equipment shed. Looking in the door, the couple saw the ball sitting right in the middle of the room. "Look," volunteered the golfer's wife, "if I hold the door open, you can play a shot from here to the green."

This struck the golfer as an interesting challenge, but alas, the ball missed the open door and struck his wife on the temple, killing her instantly.

Many years later the widower was playing with a friend when he hit the exact same slice. The two of them walked into the shed, and, sure enough, there sat the ball in the center of the room. "I tell you what," said the friend. "If I hold the door open, I bet you can get the ball back onto the green."

"Oh, no," said the golfer, shaking his head. "I tried that once before and it took me seven shots to get out."

□ □ □

A timid tourist stopped a New York City cop. "Can you tell me how to get to Carnegie Hall," she asked, clearing her throat nervously, "or should I just go fuck myself?"

□ □ □

Especially horny one night, Sam rolled over and nuzzled his wife. "How about it, honey?" he asked tenderly.

"Oh, Sam, I've got an appointment with the gynecologist tomorrow," said his wife, going on to explain that the doctor had requested that she abstain from intercourse for twenty-four hours before an appointment.

Sam sighed deeply and turned over to his side of the bed. A few minutes later he rolled back and asked hopefully, "You don't have a dental appointment, too, do you?"

□ □ □

Six-year-old Teddy came into the house with his hands cupped together and asked, "Mom, is there such a thing as boy grasshoppers?"

"Why, yes, honey. Why do you ask?"

"How about girl grasshoppers?" persisted Teddy.

Mrs. Englehardt had never discussed the birds and the bees with her son and was convinced of his complete innocence. And, not wanting to deal with the whole issue quite yet, she patted him on the head and answered, "No, dear."

"Just wondering," said Teddy, smiling sweetly. Turning away, he clapped his hands together and screamed, "FAGGOTS!"

□ □ □

Did you hear that *A&P* and *Stop & Shop* have merged?

The new store's called *Stop 'n' P.*

□ □ □

During the Indian Wars, a cavalry brigade led a charge against a tribe of Cheyenne warriors, completely decimating the Indians. At the end, the only one left alive was the Indian chief. "Since you fought so bravely," said the cavalry officer, "I'm going to spare your life."

Just as the chief was trying to find words to express his gratitude, over the hill came a mess of Indians who completely wiped out the cavalry brigade. The only survivor was the officer, to whom the Indian said, "I'm not going to be as generous as you were—you're going to die. But you can have three wishes before I kill you."

The officer nodded, thought for a minute, and said, "I'd like to see my horse." The horse was brought around, the officer whispered in its ear, and the horse tore off, only to return in an hour or so with a luscious blonde on its back.

"Please feel free to make use of my teepee," offered the chief tactfully. When the officer emerged some time later, the chief asked about his second wish.

"I'd like to see my horse." Again the horse received a whispered command and galloped off, this time returning with a lovely redhead. Again the chief gestured graciously toward his teepee, and again waited an appropriate amount of time before inquiring as to his prisoner's last wish.

"I'd like to see my horse." This time when the horse was led up to him, the officer grasped its bridle firmly, pinched its lips with his other hand, and whispered fiercely, "Watch my lips—I said p*o*sse."

□ □ □

How do married couples do it doggie-style?

Without all the licking and sniffing.

□ □ □

"Hey, buddy, can you tell me where hats are sold?" the burly guy asked the information clerk at Macy's. "I've gotta buy one for this big-headed, no-good, son-of-a-bitching son of mine," he explained, and turned to give the little boy at his side such a cuff on the ear that the kid nearly fell over.

Shocked, the information clerk directed him to the fourth floor, where the guy stopped the first salesperson in sight. "I've gotta buy a hat for this big-headed, no-good, little shit son of mine," he told him, kicking the kid in the stomach so hard that he doubled up and keeled over right in the aisle.

"Over there, to the left of the escalator," gasped the salesperson, aghast at the big man's brutality.

"I'll be glad to be of service, sir," said the salesman when the man reached the hat department, "but first I must ask you why you're beating your child like that."

"Well, I'll tell you," said the burly man, his aggressive demeanor melting away and a dreamy look coming over his face. "See, I once made myself a vow that I'd bust my ass, make plenty of money, and marry a beautiful woman with a nice, tight pussy. Well, I made a million dollars by the time I was twenty-five. Then I met this beautiful woman, and she loved me too. Then we got married, and damned if she didn't have the tightest pussy I'd ever felt. And *then* along came this big-headed . . ."

□ □ □

How can you tell when a lawyer is lying?

His lips are moving.

□ □ □

A man from the city decided to buy himself a pig, so he took a drive in the country until he came across a sign reading, "Pigs for Sale." Turning into the drive, he parked next to an old farmer standing by a pen full of pigs and explained his mission. Agreeing to a price of a dollar a pound, he picked out his pig, whereupon the old man picked up the pig by the tail with his teeth. "Ayuh," he pronounced, setting the squealing animal down, "that there pig weighs sixty-nine pounds."

Noting his customer's astonishment, the farmer explained that the ability to weigh pigs in this manner was a family trait passed down through the generations. Skeptical, and not wanting to be taken for a city slicker, the man insisted on a second opinion. So the old farmer called his son over from the barn, and the boy in the same fashion pronounced the pig's weight to be sixty-nine pounds.

Convinced, the man pulled out his wallet, but the farmer asked him to go to the farmhouse and pay his wife, who would give him a receipt. The man was gone for a long time, and when he finally returned to the pigpen it was without a receipt. "What's the problem, son?" asked the old man.

"I went up there just like you said," recounted the man from the city, "but your wife was too busy to give me a receipt."

"Too busy doing what?" wondered the farmer.

"Well, sir, I'm not exactly sure," stammered the man, "but I think she's weighing the handyman."

□ □ □

A young woman was sitting on the bus cooing to her baby when a drunk staggered aboard and down the aisle. Stopping in front of her, he looked down and pronounced, "Lady, that is the ugliest baby I have ever seen."

The woman burst into tears and there was such an outcry of sympathy among the other passengers that they kicked the drunk off. But the woman kept on sobbing and wailing, so loudly that finally the driver pulled the bus over to the side of the road. "Look, I don't know what that bum said to you," the driver told his inconsolable passenger, "but to help calm you down I'm going to get you a cup of tea." And off he went, coming back shortly with a cup of tea from the corner deli.

"Now calm down, lady," soothed the driver, "everything's going to be okay. See, I brought you a cup of nice, hot tea, and I even got a banana for your pet monkey."

□ □ □

What's dumb?

Directions on toilet paper.

What's dumber than that?

Reading them.

Even dumber?

Reading them and learning something.

Dumbest of all?

Reading them and having to correct something you've been doing wrong.

□ □ □

An anthropologist had been studying an obscure Thai hill tribe when he contracted a particularly virulent case of jungle rot and was dead in a week. His heartbroken widow accompanied the casket back to Milwaukee, where she invited his three best friends to attend an intimate funeral. When the brief service was over, she asked each of the friends to place an offering in the casket, as had been the custom of the tribe he had been living with. "It would mean a great deal to Herbie," she said, then broke down into racking sobs.

Moved to tears himself, the first friend, a doctor, gently deposited $100 in the coffin.

Dabbing his cheeks, the second friend, a stockbroker, laid $150 on the deceased Herbie's pillow.

The third friend, a lawyer, wrote a check for $450, put it in the casket, and pocketed the cash.

□ □ □

The nearest customer was five stools away, but that didn't keep Josh from leaning over toward the bartender and commenting, "Geez, there's a lousy smell in here." A few minutes later he added, "It smells just like . . . shit." Puzzled by the origin of the stench, he moved closer to the other customer, and sure enough the smell worsened. "Phew, you really stink," he pointed out.

"I know," said the man apologetically. "It's because of my job." Seeing that Josh was interested in a further explanation, he went on, "I'm with an elephant act, and before each show I have to give the elephant an enema so he doesn't take a dump during the performance. Frankly, it's a tricky business, because I have to administer it quickly and then jump back. And sometimes I just don't move fast enough."

"Jesus," commiserated Josh, shaking his head. "How much do they pay you for this lousy job?"

"Eighty-five bucks a week," said the man cheerfully.

"You've got to be kidding. Why don't you quit?"

"What?" retorted the man, "and get out of show business?"

□ □ □

Define "egghead":

What Mrs. Dumpty gives to Humpty.

□ □ □

A fellow was having a few beers at his local pub on a Saturday afternoon when he was approached by a man dressed all in green. "Know what?" the man in green asked confidingly. "I'm a leprechaun, and I'm feeling extremely generous. So generous, in fact, that I'm willing to grant you any three wishes you'd like."

"No kidding! Gee, that's great," blurted the lucky fellow. "I could sure use some extra cash."

"No problem," said the leprechaun with a gracious wave. "The trunk of your car is now crammed with hundred-dollar bills. What's next?"

"Well, I wouldn't mind moving to a nicer house."

"Consider it done," announced the leprechaun grandly. "Four bedrooms, three-and-a-half baths, up on Society Hill. And your third wish?"

"Well, uh, how about a gorgeous blonde?" suggested the fellow, blushing a bit.

"She's in your new house, waiting for you in a flimsy negligee."

"This is really great," said the lucky guy, getting down from his stool and starting for the door. "I wish there were some way to thank you."

"Oh, but there is," spoke up the man in green. "I'd like a blow job."

"A blow job?" The man wasn't sure he'd heard right.

"Yup. And after all I've given you, it doesn't seem like much to ask, now does it?

The lucky fellow had to admit this was true, so in a dark corner of the bar he obliged his benefactor. As he pulled on his jacket and turned away, the man in green stopped him. "Just one question," he asked. "How old are you?"

"Thirty-four."

"And at your age you still believe in leprechauns?"

□ □ □

The slovenly, obese Hollywood agent got up from his seat at the comedy club to go to the bathroom. Returning with Perrier and popcorn in hand, he inquired of a young woman, "Did I step on your foot a few minutes ago?"

"As a matter of fact you did," she replied tartly.

"Great! Then that's my table."

□ □ □

The hooker came up to the single man at the bar and said boldly, "I cost three hundred dollars—and I'm worth it."

"Is that so?" asked the fellow, looking her over. "Three hundred bucks is a lot of money."

Snuggling up so that he could smell her perfume and leaning over so he could appreciate her cleavage, the hooker proceeded to elaborate upon the skills, the techniques, the talent and imagination she brought to her trade. "I'll make love to you like you've never been made love to before," she promised with a throaty chuckle. "In fact, whisper any three words—picture your wildest fantasy coming true—and I'll make it happen."

"Any three words? For three hundred dollars?" he asked, perking up considerably.

"That's right, baby," confirmed the prostitute, blowing him a pouty little kiss.

"We've got a deal," cried the new client happily. He pulled her up onto his lap, pulled her long blond hair away from her ear, and whispered, "Paint my house."

□ □ □

What do a blow job and eggs Benedict have in common?

They're the only two things you never get at home.

□ □ □

When Mike showed up for his appointment with the urologist, the doctor informed him a sperm sample was necessary, and instructed him to go to Room Four. Dutifully going down the hall, Mike opened the door to Room Four and found two absolutely gorgeous women clad in scanty lingerie. They proceeded to arouse him beyond his wildest dreams, and Mike headed back down the hall with a dreamy smile and a *terrific* sperm sample.

Realizing he had to pee, Mike opened the door to the first bathroom he came across, only to interrupt a guy frantically beating off with a copy of *Hustler*. In the second bathroom a fellow was busy masturbating with the company of the *Penthouse* centerfold. Back in the doctor's office and curious as hell, Mike couldn't resist asking the doctor about the other two fellows.

"Oh, those guys?" asked the doctor dismissively. "Those're my Medicaid patients."

□ □ □

When Alec was informed by his doctor that he had only twelve more hours to live, he rushed home and told his wife, who collapsed in racking sobs. But then she pulled herself together, clasped his hands in hers, and promised, "Then I'm going to make tonight the best night of your life, darling." She went out and bought all his favorite delicacies, opened a bottle of fine champagne, served him dinner dressed in his favorite sexy peignoir, and led him up to bed, where she made passionate love to him.

Just as they were about to fall asleep, Alec tapped her on the shoulder. "Honey, could we make love again?"

"Sure, sweetheart," she said sleepily, and obliged.

"Once more, baby?" he asked afterward. "It's our last night together."

"Mmmhmm," she mumbled, and they made love a third time.

"One last time, darling," he begged a little later, shaking her by the shoulders.

"Fine!" she snapped. "After all, what do you care? *You* don't have to get up in the morning."

□ □ □

Did you hear about the new restaurant that just opened up on the moon?

Good food, but *no* atmosphere.

□ □ □

The psychiatrist closed his notebook, clasped his hands in satisfaction, and contemplated the patient sitting across from him. "I confess that in my profession one seldom speaks of 'cures,' Miss Kamin," he said sagely, "but at this time I am very pleased to be able to pronounce you one hundred percent cured. Goodbye, and good luck."

"Swell," muttered the woman, looking downcast and beginning to pout. "That's just swell."

The psychiatrist was taken by surprise. "Miss Kamin, I thought you'd be delighted. What on earth is wrong?"

"Oh, it's fine for you," snapped Miss Kamin, "but look at it from my side. Three years ago I was Joan of Arc. Now I'm nobody."

□ □ □

A rape victim, Marcella was mortified by the prospect of testifying against her attacker, but friends and family convinced her of her obligations. So the case came to trial, and at a certain point, the DA asked her what the defendant had said before the alleged assault. Blushing, Marcella requested permission to write out the answer rather than say it aloud. And after reading the note, the judge instructed that it be passed along to the members of the jury.

When the note reached the last juror, who was sound asleep, he was woken by an elbow from the woman next to him. She passed him the note, which read, "I'm going to fuck you like you've never been fucked before, sweetmeat." The juror grinned broadly, and slipped the note into his pocket.

"Will juror number twelve kindly pass the note back to the bench?" requested the judge.

"Oh, Your Honor, I couldn't," he stammered. "It's too personal."

□ □ □

"Tell me the truth, Doctor Hill," said the emaciated fellow. "How much longer am I going to live?"

"It's always hard to predict," she replied brightly, "but let's just say that if I were you, I wouldn't start watching any miniseries on TV."

Too Tasteless to Be Included

What would Hitler have invented if he'd lived another six months?

The self-cleaning oven.

□ □ □

Why are blacks so quick on their feet?

Because they spend their first nine months dodging coat hangers.

□ □ □

When his girlfriend died suddenly, Jimmy was truly distraught. When the truck came to take her off to the morgue, he pulled the attendant aside and asked if he could pay a final visit to his beloved.

"Sure," said the guy, but indicated it would cost him.

Jimmy readily agreed, handed over the money at the morgue, and was shown to the room where her corpse lay on an autopsy table. "God, I'd really like to kiss her one more time," he admitted wistfully. The attendant named a price, and though he was getting short on cash, Jimmy readily handed it over.

After the kiss, Jimmy looked up with tears in his eyes and confessed that he still found her incredibly attractive, so much so that he desperately wanted to do it with her one more time.

Nervous about someone coming in, the attendant was reluctant to give in to Jimmy's last request. Finally they agreed that in return for the last of Jimmy's cash, he would cut out the relevant part of the woman's anatomy and let Jimmy take it home. Finishing the job, the attendant turned to Jimmy and asked if he'd like it wrapped up.

"No, thank you," answered Jimmy. "I'll eat it here."

□ □ □

If a truckload of dead babies is gross, and a live one at the bottom eating its way out is grosser than gross, what's grossest of all?

When he goes back for seconds.

□ □ □

And what have you got when you cover four dead babies with a piece of glass?

A coffee table.

□ □ □

"What's the trouble, sonny?" asked the kindly old gent of the little boy crying his heart out on the curb.

"A drunk puked over there," sobbed the boy, "and my brother Phil's getting all the big pieces."

"Never mind," said the old man consolingly, pulling out his wallet. "Here's a dollar. Go buy a loaf of bread and you can sop up the juice."

□ □ □

"Mommy, Mommy, why are you moaning?"

"Shut up and keep licking!"

□ □ □

"Mommy, Mommy, what's an Oedipus complex?"

"Shut up and kiss me."

□ □ □

Why do husbands abuse their wives?

Why not?

□ □ □

One night Lloyd and Lois were playing one of their favorite games in bed: fart football. Lloyd went first with a trumpeting fart. "Seven points," he declared proudly.

Lois's slightly less stentorian effort was only good for five, but within a few seconds Lloyd granted her the extra two points for pungency.

On it went, until the score reached 28–21, with Lloyd in the lead. Fiercely competitive, Lois strained and groaned until she was red in the face and until—to her considerable dismay—she shat right in the bed. She thought for a moment, then grinned and announced: "Halftime! Change sides."

□ □ □

What do you do when you see six white guys beating up a black guy?

Laugh.

Then what?

Yell, "He raped my sister!"

□ □ □

Why are babies born with soft spots on top of their heads?

So that if there's a fire in the hospital, the nurse can carry out five with each hand.

□ □ □

Did you hear about the fellow who chewed his baby's toes off?

He forgot his wife was pregnant.

□ □ □

Two fishermen were accustomed to fishing alongside one another every weekend but they never exchanged any words. Then, one weekend, one of them failed to appear. Nor did he show the next weekend. But on the third Saturday, he was back in his usual spot.

"Missed you," said the first fisherman.

"Got married."

Half an hour later the first one said, "She must be something to keep you off fishing for two weekends. Is she that beautiful?"

"Nothing special," said the newlywed.

Half an hour later the first man spoke up again. "She a good cook?"

"If you like frozen food."

In due course came the next question. "She must be dynamite in bed then, eh?"

"Same as all the rest," said the second fisherman, shrugging offhandedly.

"So why'd you marry her?" demanded the first, unable to contain himself.

"She's got worms—and I just *love* to fish."